DOWNLOAD
NEW YORK STATE OF MIND 1.0
FREE!

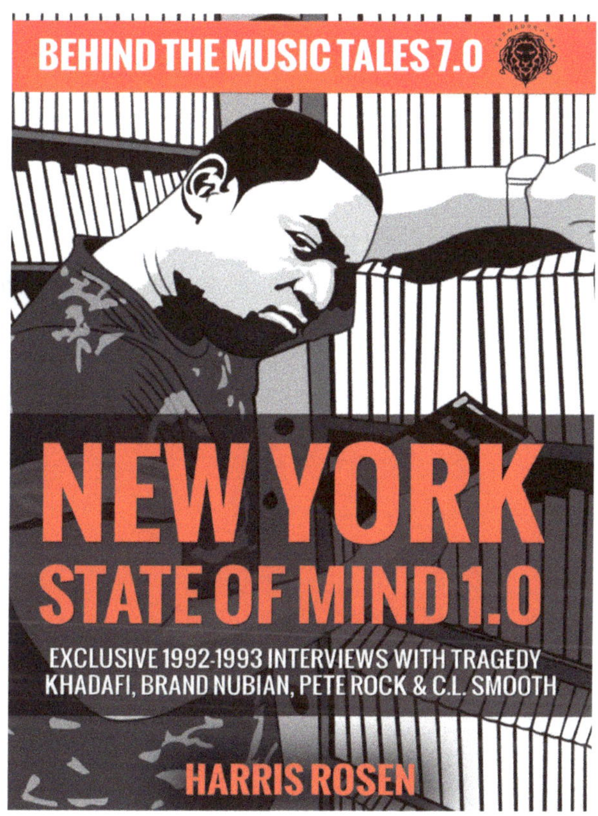

There are hundreds of interviews and dozens of *Behind The Music Tales* series books to follow.

That's why I am giving you a copy of *New York State of Mind 1.0* for FREE!

Get exclusive 1992 and 1993 interviews with Tragedy Khadafi, Brand Nubian, and Pete Rock & C.L. Smooth FREE!

I am only looking for your email. You will receive emails with updates on new releases, exclusive images, original audio, and be eligible for free advance copies of series books. You can opt out at any time.

http://eepurl.com/cj-cvb

Behind The Music Tales Books

N.W.A: The Aftermath

The Real Eminem: Broke City Trash Rapper

The Real Destiny's Child: The Writing's On The Wall

New York State of Mind 1.0

The Reasonings of Buju Banton, Bounty Killer & Sizzla

Magnolia: Home of tha Soldiers
(Behind the Scenes with the Cash Money Millionaires)

The Real 213

The Real MC Eiht: Geah!

The Real Diddy

The Real Daft Punk

Praise for Harris Rosen

This guy! I plead the fifth. This guy is nuts."
- Eminem

"Dope questions, man. Very insightful, very thoughtful."
- Guru (Gang Starr)

"You like a Psychiatrist or some shit? This shit is just coming out but go ahead."
- Mary J. Blige

"Definitely a real interview! Digging deep up in there, man. Not afraid to ask questions!"
- K-Ci Hailey (Jodeci)

"The Wizard asked me for a copy of your magazine."
- Guy-Manuel de Homem-Christo (Daft Punk)

"You didn't wear your glasses and you haven't carried your hearing aid. What else is wrong with you?"
- Bushwick Bill

"Peace and blessing, Brother Harris. Thank you for inspiring my words. Keep 'yo balance."
- Erykah Badu

"Can I see that pen?"
- Bobby Brown

"What else do you want to know? Talk to me."
- Aaliyah

The Real Destiny's Child:
The Writing's On The Wall

Exclusive Interviews with
Beyoncé Knowles, Kelly Rowland,
LeToya Luckett, and LaTavia Roberson

Harris Rosen

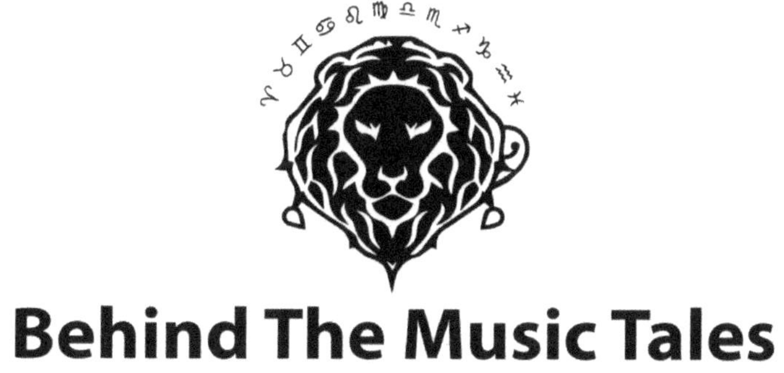

Behind The Music Tales

Published by Peace! Carving

2nd edition

First published as a Digital Edition in December 2015

This print edition first published in August 2016

ISBN: 978-0-9812587-4-4 (Print)

ISBN: 978-0-9812587-5-1 (Digital)

Mr. Heller Press

Heller HQ

QB
Spadina-Fort York Toronto, ON M5V 2B3 Canada

Dedication

This series is dedicated to my son Louis, late father, mother, sister, grandmother & the late Raymond Wallace.

Thank you for a lifetime of support and encouragement. I would not be here without you.

Acknowledgments

I wish to personally thank the following people for their contributions to my inspiration and knowledge and other help in creating this book. Mark Reed, Rob Harris, Peter Cherniawski, Joey DAMMIT!, Ian Steaman, Director X, Taj Critchlow, Eon Sinclair, Jr., Todd DeKoker, Phil Demetro, James Watt, Chandler Bolt, William J. Genereux, Peter Lazanik, Rishi Persaud.

Table of Contents

DESTINY'S
CHILD
04:09:04:09.   KR.34.3335 0608+0962

PREFACE

FLASHBACK

It's like your sister. We're just like sisters. Sisters get into arguments, but eventually, they talk about things. I mean, it's like our love is deeper than this group and it's deeper than an argument. You might be mad for a day or two, but we get over it.

- Beyoncé Knowles

Destiny's Child was groomed from elementary school age to flourish in the music business. Every little step skillfully crafted from choreographed dance routines and image through the music and lyrics. By design they launched November 11, 1997, with the infectious uptempo "No, No, No (Part 2)" featuring Sony first guest assassin Wyclef Jean. It served to introduce them to the world in style hitting number 3 on the U.S. Billboard Hot 100 and selling over 1 million copies. The debut self-titled album, **Destiny's Child**, followed on February 17, 1998, it maintained the young quartet's warm reception by selling over 1 million copies and earning Best R&B/Soul Album at the Soul Train Lady of Soul Awards. It was an excellent launch and interest was piqued.

When it came time to create the sophomore album, **The Writing's On The Wall**, it was an entirely different landscape. The Columbia arm of Sony Music spared no expense and retained the best of the best to CO-create a nonstop brigade of hits while inviting the girls themselves to write and produce too. The result was out of this world, and Sony Music was overjoyed. Destiny's Child became the agenda, and they smelled money, lots and lots of money.

This in-person interview with Destiny's Child occurred in a Philadelphia, Pa., hotel room in May 1999. **The Writing's On The Wall** was on the release schedule for July 27, 1999.

Destiny's Child was set to return in style and was widely forecast to land within the upper echelon of female vocal groups.

Moving up three notches, Destiny's Child features their unique vocals and phrasings throughout the album. Decide to savour the fresh southern juice on "Jumpin' Jumpin'" or dive deep into "Say My Name" it's all good. A slumber party chock full of personal family and friend secrets naturally flowing from mushy to real, the album instantaneously matures into a smooth conceptual piece on relationships that illustrates their own growth from girls to young women while speaking to a generation of young females.

Destiny's Child had a more profound love for each other. There was no talk of Beyoncé Knowles leaving the group. There was not even a hint of a whisper LeToya Luckett, and LaTavia Roberson would be unceremoniously replaced in February 2000 by Michelle Williams and Farrah Franklin. Destiny's Child embodied young and innocent happy teenagers, close friends lounging side-by-side on a king-size bed.

The Writing's On The Wall recorded over a two month period that was nine years in the making. Destiny's Child CO-wrote on 11 songs. Beyoncé Knowles produced vocal arrangements, melodies and lyrics. The All-star production team delivered hits. LeToya Luckett, LaTavia Roberson, Kelly Rowland and Beyoncé Knowles sat on the verge of breaking through to the masses.

***

Destiny's Child was destined for stardom. Beyoncé Knowles won her first school talent show in 1988 at the age of seven. By the age of nine, she was a member of the sextet Girl's Tyme with LaTavia Roberson, signing, dancing and rapping on the Houston talent show circuit. Kelly Rowland joined the ranks in 1992. In 1993, at the age of 12, they performed to a national television audience of millions on America's largest talent show, Star Search. Sadly they lost.

A devastating blow with knockout potential, Beyoncé's father, Matthew Knowles, surveyed the damage and went all in. He quit his job, took over the reins full-time and never looked back. The group was cut down to four members. Tamar Davis, who went on to sing with Prince and feature on The Voice, and LaTavia Roberson's cousins Nikki and Nina Taylor were ousted. LeToya Luckett was added, and they set to work as a quartet practising routines and performing in backyards and Beyonce's mother's Headliners Salon. Spending summers in intensive "boot camp" vocal and dance lessons.

They changed names a few times using Something Fresh, Cliché, the Dolls, and then Destiny before landing a deal with Elektra Records in 1995. A video for "One Time" featuring Beyoncé and LaTavia was filmed, and then they were unceremoniously dropped by the end of the year. It is quite possibly the most massive A&R misstep of all-time.

Matthew Knowles regrouped and the next year Destiny's Child signed with Columbia Records. "Killing Time" on the **Men In Black** soundtrack marked their major label debut on July 1, 1997. "No No No" followed on November 11, 1997, and the **Destiny's Child** album on February 18, 1998.

Beyoncé Knowles, LaTavia Roberson, Kelly Rowland and LeToya Luckett had been friends since they met in elementary school back in 1990 at the age of nine. Growing up together during their most formative years mutually engaged and locked on the same goal, they became sisters. Nine years later, with the imminent release of **The Writing's On The Wall**, their destiny was finally fixed to manifest.

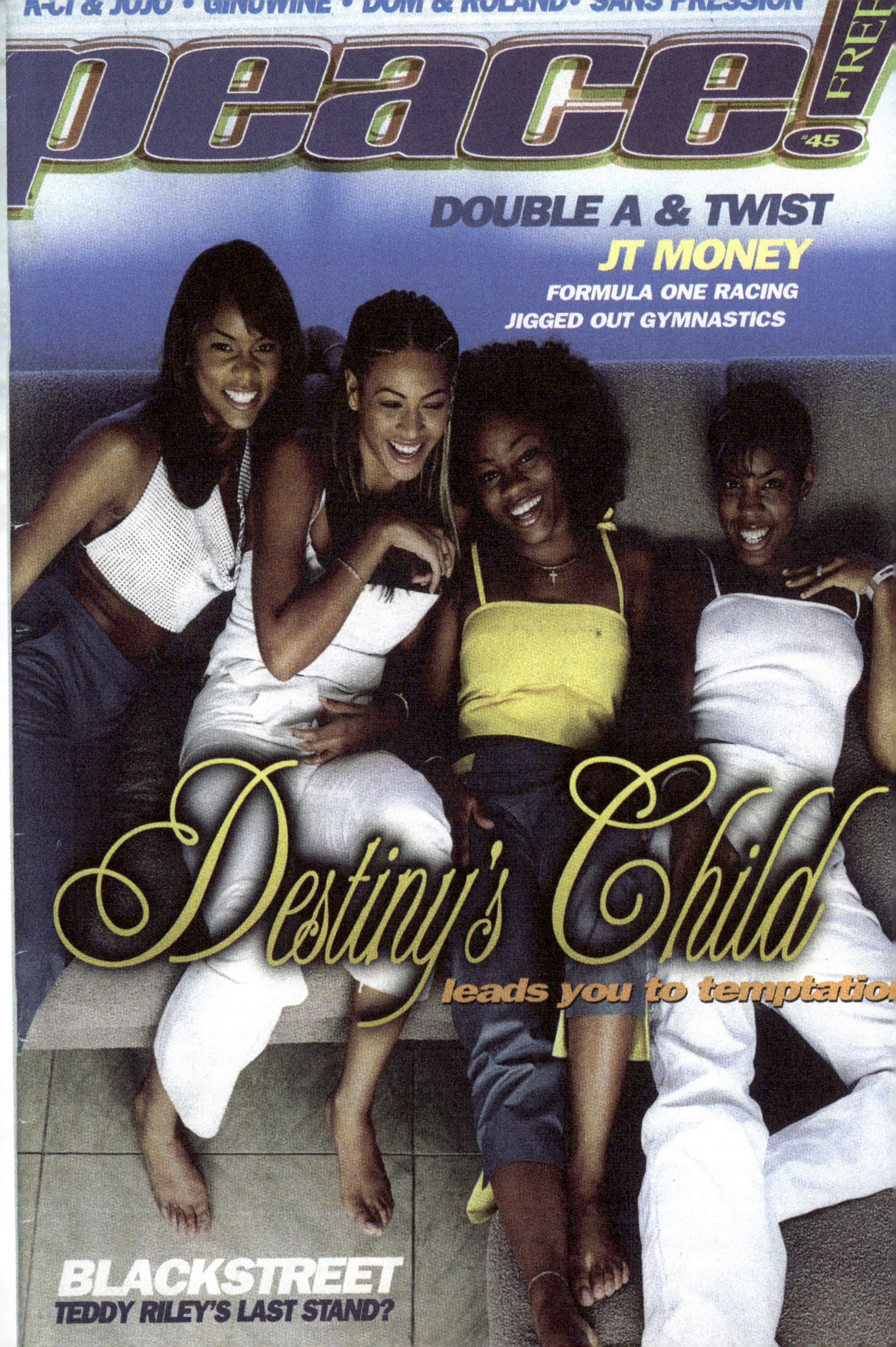
K-CI & JOJO • GINUWINE • DOM & ROLAND• SANS PRESSION
peace!
FREE
#45
DOUBLE A & TWIST
JT MONEY
FORMULA ONE RACING
JIGGED OUT GYMNASTICS
Destiny's Child
leads you to temptation
BLACKSTREET
TEDDY RILEY'S LAST STAND?

PHILADELPHIA, PA - SPRING 1999

The Writing's On The Wall is a cliché. We thought it was a very positive cliché. It means that something big is about to happen.

- LaTavia Roberson

Ring... Ring... Ring... "Hello?"

The Director of PR for Sony Music Canada is on the line proposing a Destiny's Child cover story feature. We exchange pleasantries and discussed the opportunity. Destiny's Child had sold over 1 million copies of their debut self-titled album, **Destiny's Child**, and a new album was in the pipeline. They were now a high priority for the label with the requisite big-money push in the wings. An advance copy of **The Writing's On The Wall** couriered over, and it only took one listen to discover it was a smash. Song after song these four young belles from Houston, Texas, delivering hit after hit and I instantly visualised them sitting on top of the charts for a long time to come. Terms were outlined, and I officially landed the in-person Canadian print exclusive.

Behind the scenes industry talk had already begun. Beyoncé was groomed for a solo career, and her destiny was to be similar to that of none other than Diana Ross. Ross had led the charge for Motown's The Supremes, the world's most successful vocal group, as the founding member and lead singer before parting way and carving out a considerable solo career in music with combined sales exceeding 100 million copies. She went on to star in feature films. Billboard magazine named her the female entertainer of the 20th Century. Alongside The Supremes, she was inducted into the Rock N' Roll Hall of Fame. She received the Grammy Lifetime Achievement Award in 2012. You may know her performer daughter, Tracee Ellis Ross, who currently stars on TV's **Black-ish**.

Flights were booked, and the label Marketing Manager, Craig "Big C" Mannix, and I jetted into Philadelphia, Pa, where the group based for the day in advance promotional duties. Upon checking-in to the hotel, we connected with their Road Manager who escorted us to their room.

LaTavia Roberson, LeToya Luckett, Kelly Rowland and Beyoncé Knowles greeted us at the door. My first impression was that they were young, and it became instantly apparent that they were close friends and confidants. Casually dressed and with no make-up or stylist in sight, forthwith their positive energy took over as they introduced themselves to us. C left with the Road Manager and there I was alone in the room with Destiny's Child. All four of them posted up on the bed together, side-by-side, listening attentively to my questions and chiming in over each other to get in a response.

Destiny's Child projected an air of confidence, and there was a sense of anticipation in the air. **The Writing's On The Wall** was complete. Its soon-to-be-unveiled leadoff single "Bills, Bills, Bills" a few weeks away on the release schedule slated for a June 14, 1999, release.

Beyoncé spoke on her love and appreciation of the group's European fan base and mentioned she was interested in acting. The group discussed their maturation from girls to young women. A new "colourful website" was hyped a few times. There was an underlying tone to respect their business acumen and to take them seriously as artists and adults.

LeToya Luckett, LaTavia Roberson, Kelly Rowland and Beyoncé Knowles had grown up together in the group performing as sisters and Destiny's Child were in sync

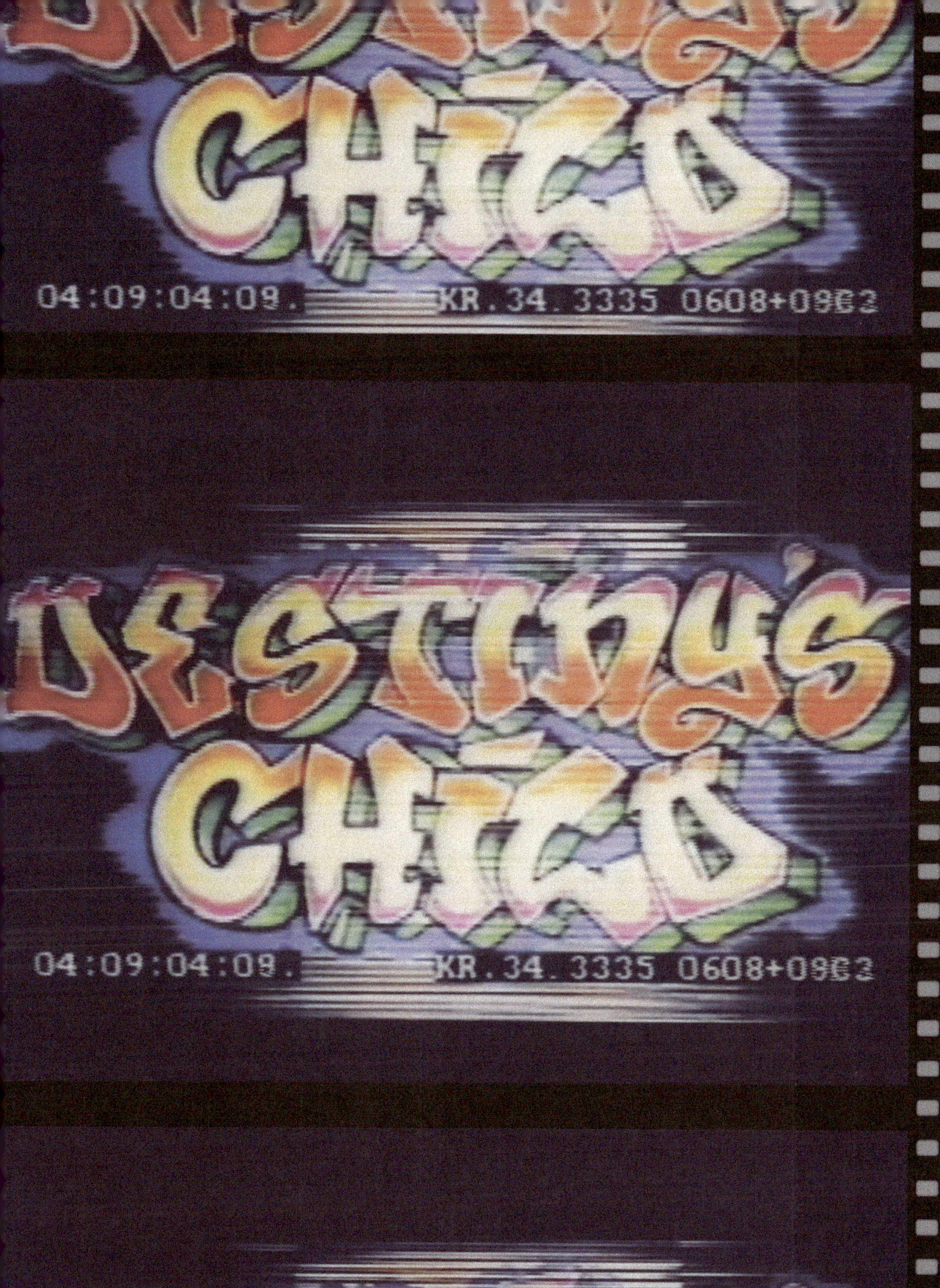

DESTINY'S
CHILD
04:09:04:09.   KR. 34. 3335 0608+0962
DESTINY'S
CHILD
04:09:04:09.   KR. 34. 3335 0608+0963
DESTINY'S

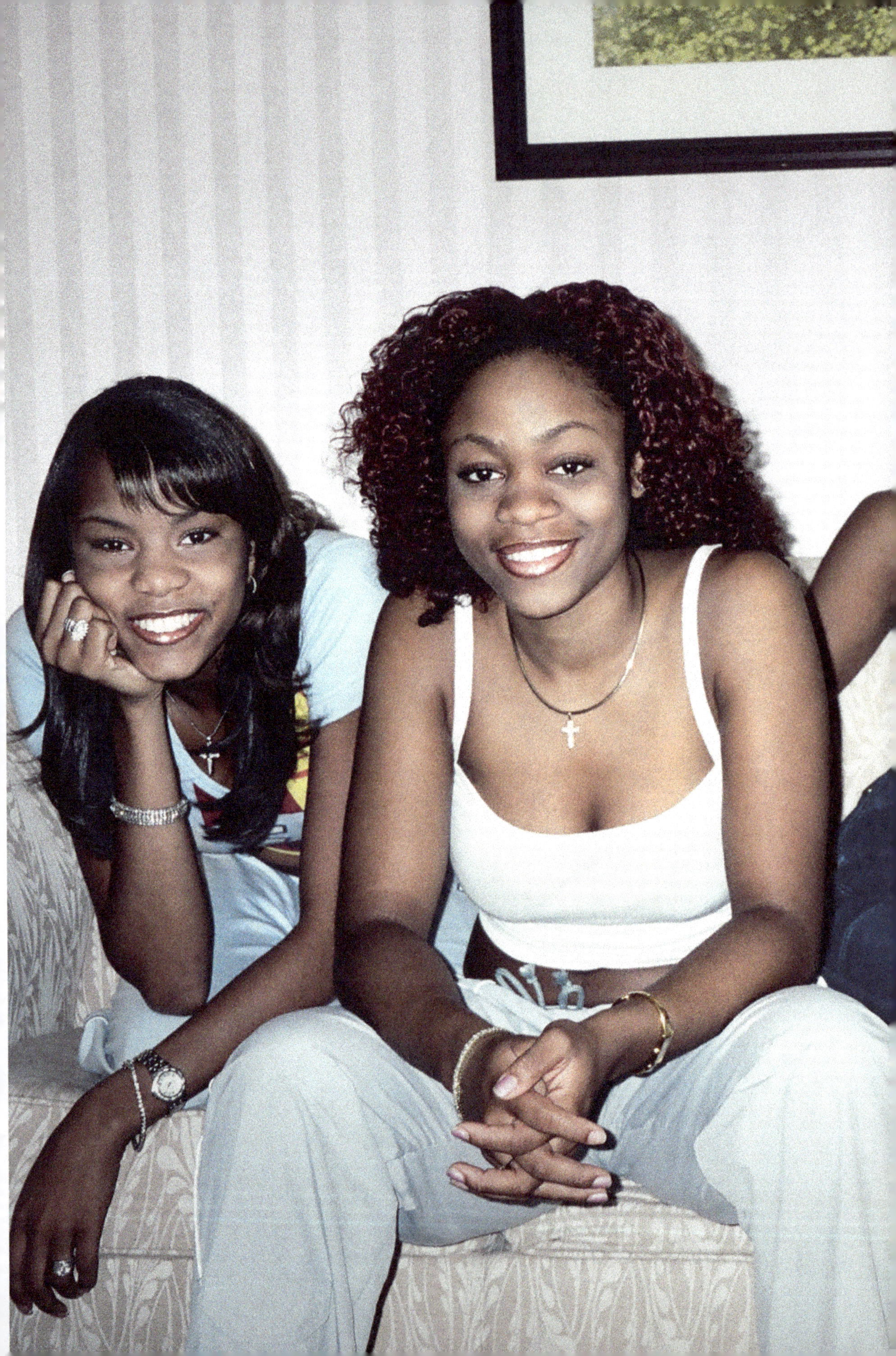

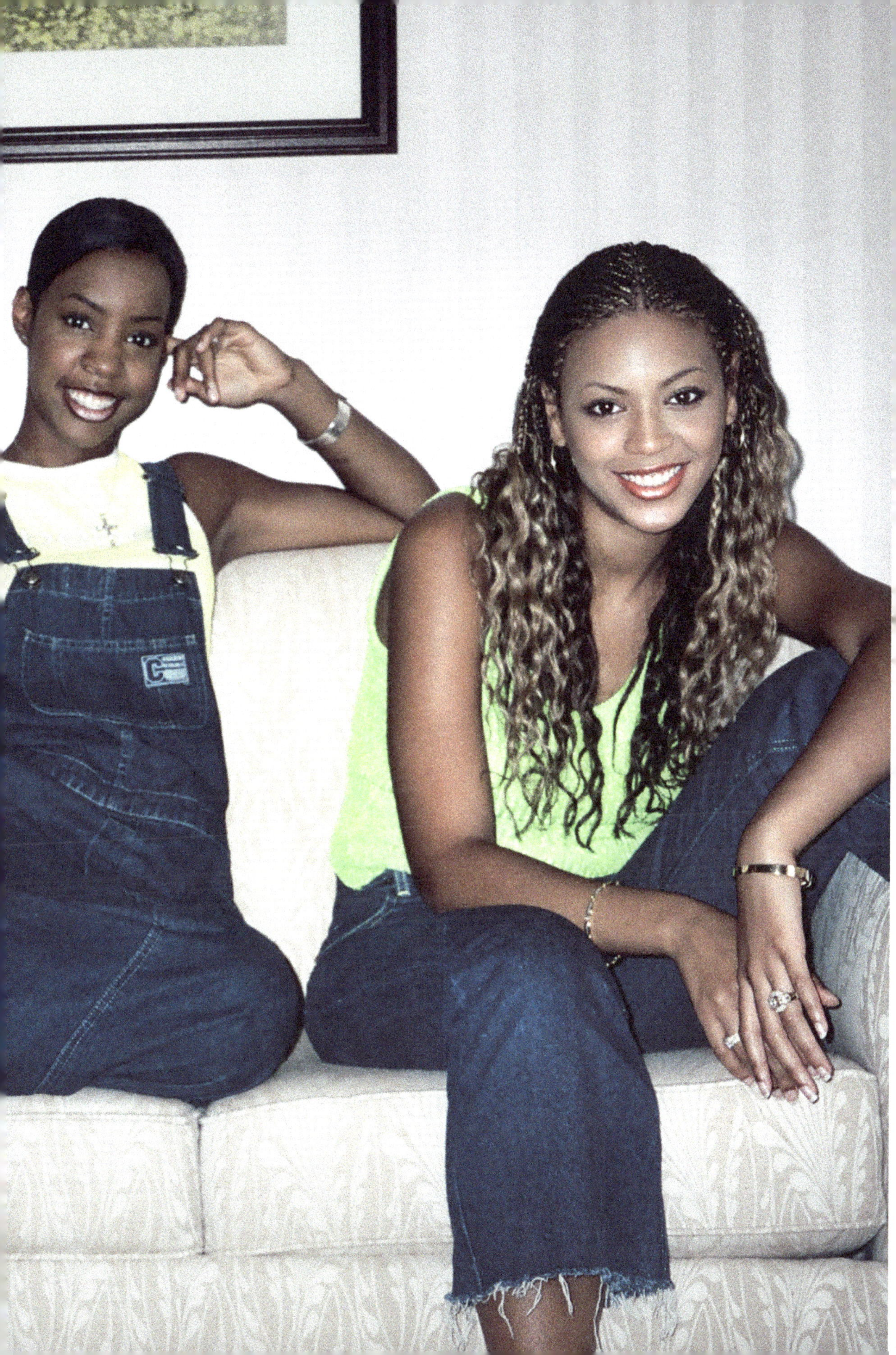

THE INTERVIEW

Hi, I'm LeToya.

I'm LaTavia.

I'm Kelly.

I'm Beyoncé.

Break it all down. What's it all about?

Kelly Rowland:

Well, we just finished recording our sophomore album.

Beyoncé Knowles:

Actually, we finished recording it a little while back. It only took two months as opposed to the first album; it took two years. We got a chance to work with some great producers; She'kspere (Briggs) and Kandi (Burruss), who did "No Scrubs". Also D'wayne Wiggins, who did a lot of the first album; Rodney Jerkins, Daryl Simmons, Missy Elliott, and Chad Elliot, who did a remix with "Next" and... LeToya Luckett: Track Masterz and Sporty Thievz is also rapping on -

Beyoncé Knowles:

"Bills". But we got a chance to write on 11 of the songs, and I got the chance to produce on a lot of the songs. So this album it comes a lot - a lot more from us. We've matured since the last album vocally, and just from girls to young ladies. We wanted to showcase that in the album. So we talked about more mature subjects, and we just thought it was very important to us to write, so what we sing about we can relate to and so we can feel, and you can get a better feel for what we're about after listening to the album.

What are you all about?

Kelly Rowland:

Destiny's Child is all about performing.

Beyoncé Knowles:

Yeah, performing and entertaining.

Kelly Rowland:

We thought that this album we wanted to move up a notch and started writing like Beyoncé said because there's always room for growing and learning in the industry. So, we're about performing, we're about giving our fans a good show, and just moving up the next level always.

LeToya Luckett:

I think entertaining too.

Beyoncé Knowles:

I mean, we want to get into acting in the future. We got a chance to do the Smart Guy, one episode, and that was a lot of fun. So we want to do more of that. Right now we're concentrating on promoting this second album, that's what we're doing now. We're going around doing radio shows and retail and stores and things like that to try to promote this new album.

Kelly Rowland:

Letting people know about the new album and how excited we are about the new album.

LaTavia Roberson:

Which will be in stores July 27.

Beyoncé Knowles:

The name of it is **The Writing's on the Wall**.

What's the writing? I don't see any writing on the wall.

LaTavia Roberson:

The writing's on the wall is a cliché. We thought it was a very positive cliché. It means that something big is about to happen. It's obvious that something is about to happen, and our album is the majority - All of the songs are about life and relationships and sides of love and life that people don't talk about. There's always talk about 'How much I love my baby,' whatever, whatever. But they don't talk about 'Yeah, but sometimes he be creeping with another woman...'

Kelly Rowland:

Or he cheated on me, or you cheated on him.

LaTavia Roberson:

You know what I'm saying!

Beyoncé Knowles:

But really, I don't think the album is about cheating on.

LaTavia Roberson:

I said some of the songs. But it is like how sometimes about how you just can't let go, it's just about relationships. And the album *The Writing's On The Wall* is saying that something big is about to happen in the relationship. And we also found that it is a good title because we have high expectations for this album, and we think this album is going to be successful, so we thought that was a good title for the album.

LeToya Luckett:

I think one of the things that separate the album from the rest of the albums that I've heard is the fact that they're not talking about the average thing and we tell a story in each song. Each song has a concept, and the album is very conceptual. We didn't want to talk about the normal stuff. So we sat around and said 'Okay, well you're in a relationship, what's going on? What's the stuff that goes on every day?' And we thought about stuff like "Temptations" and "Say My Name" and all the subjects that we talked about.

Kelly Rowland:

And also what separates this album from the last album, is that it's a new sound. The fact that we went and we got a different Producer because that's what we told the record label that we wanted a different Producer, and someone that was new that could bring Destiny's Child something new. Because if you look at a list of other artists, such as Brandy or Monica or Aaliyah, they all got like Timbaland, Keith Crouch, Rodney Jerkins, you know what I'm saying? They brought in new Producers and there was a new sound. We think that your fans respect you a lot more and they'll be able to point you out of all the groups and other artists that are out there and be like 'That's Destiny's Child! We know that sound from anywhere.' So that's what we wanted to tell them.

Who came up with the idea? Did you have a meeting and say what are we going to talk about on the album? Or did some guy punk you off and you had to write an album about him?

LeToya Luckett:

No! This is LeToya. I think She'kspere set that off. Kandi Burruss, who also CO-wrote on half the songs, well, all of the songs -

From Xscape?

LeToya Luckett:

Yeah, from Xscape, who wrote on all the songs with us with She'kspere. The first one that we did was "Bug A Boo", and we was like 'Hey, that concept is tight.'

And the more songs we did with them, the more that subject came that it wasn't about the mushy stuff, it was about the real side and what people go through. So we was like hey, let's do the whole album like that. It wasn't something that we just sat around the table and was like 'You know what, I'm sick of hearing them mushy songs, I'm sick of doing this, we going to do the real side.' Nothing like that. We just - it was a gradual thing.

Beyoncé Knowles:

It kind of like just went along that way. I mean, it just happened sort of in the studio like LeToya said. We just started writing, and one thing started leading to another, and all the songs came out like that, which is good because that gives people a little bit of something to talk about and that's what we want to do.

LaTavia Roberson:

And what's so tight is that the album is so real and none of the songs are about the same thing. They're all about a different subject. Or something that you can do to make a relationship better. Something that if you don't do the relationship is going to fall apart. It's just real tight that all of the songs they're not about the same subjects at all. But the concept of the album is the same.

The question you're going to get from everybody is what do you know about relationships at this point in your lives?

Beyoncé Knowles:

Well, we are 18.

LaTavia Roberson:

A lot of people tend to underestimate teenagers and sometimes what they go through... I mean, you go through relationships, a guy's cheating on you or y'all haven't communicated, and that relationship went wrong. I mean, it's all...

LeToya Luckett:

You're tempted to cheat on your boyfriend.

LaTavia Roberson:

Everything that we talk about we wrote. So we have to be able to relate to it if we helped write it.

LeToya Luckett:

We didn't go through every single thing, but we have friends and family members that would come to us for advice when they went through it. So, it's like you're going through it with them. It's like you're writing in their shoes and you can understand enough to write about it. You're involved enough to write about it.

Did any of the people you talked about hear the album?

Kelly Rowland:

No. We're not talking about specific guys.

LeToya Luckett:

We're only talking about the people that we went through this stuff with. Well, my friend, a friend of mine that has experienced a lot of stuff that I have been through with her, she came to the studio a couple of times while we were recording...

Beyoncé Knowles:

I know I experienced "Say My Name." I was thinking about that two performances ago when we were onstage. I was like 'Yo!' And that's like when you start getting into the song. I mean, you feel the song when you write it. But when you actually put yourself in the song shoes and like actually think about what you singing about and everything, it's even more - don't want to say it's even better.

LeToya Luckett:

I experienced a couple of songs on the album too.

Which ones?

LeToya Luckett:

"I Think He's Got To Go", "Temptations"...

Beyoncé Knowles:

I think every woman has experienced "He's Got To Go".

LeToya Luckett:

"Say My Name", I've experienced almost every song on the album. I don't think I've gotten so deep as to he's living with me because I haven't lived with a guy, so I haven't experienced that living together thing, or what might take place in that relationship.

LaTavia Roberson:

Especially when your family comes in, and they tell you-

LeToya Luckett:

Like the "Bills" thing. I think we have experienced that but to a certain point. I don't think that taking the car and not filling the car back up, stuff like that. Ain't no man ever use my car 'cause first of all, I ain't got one.

Beyoncé Knowles:

Because some guys still like on a date, they're like -

LaTavia Roberson:

Oh, not bring money.

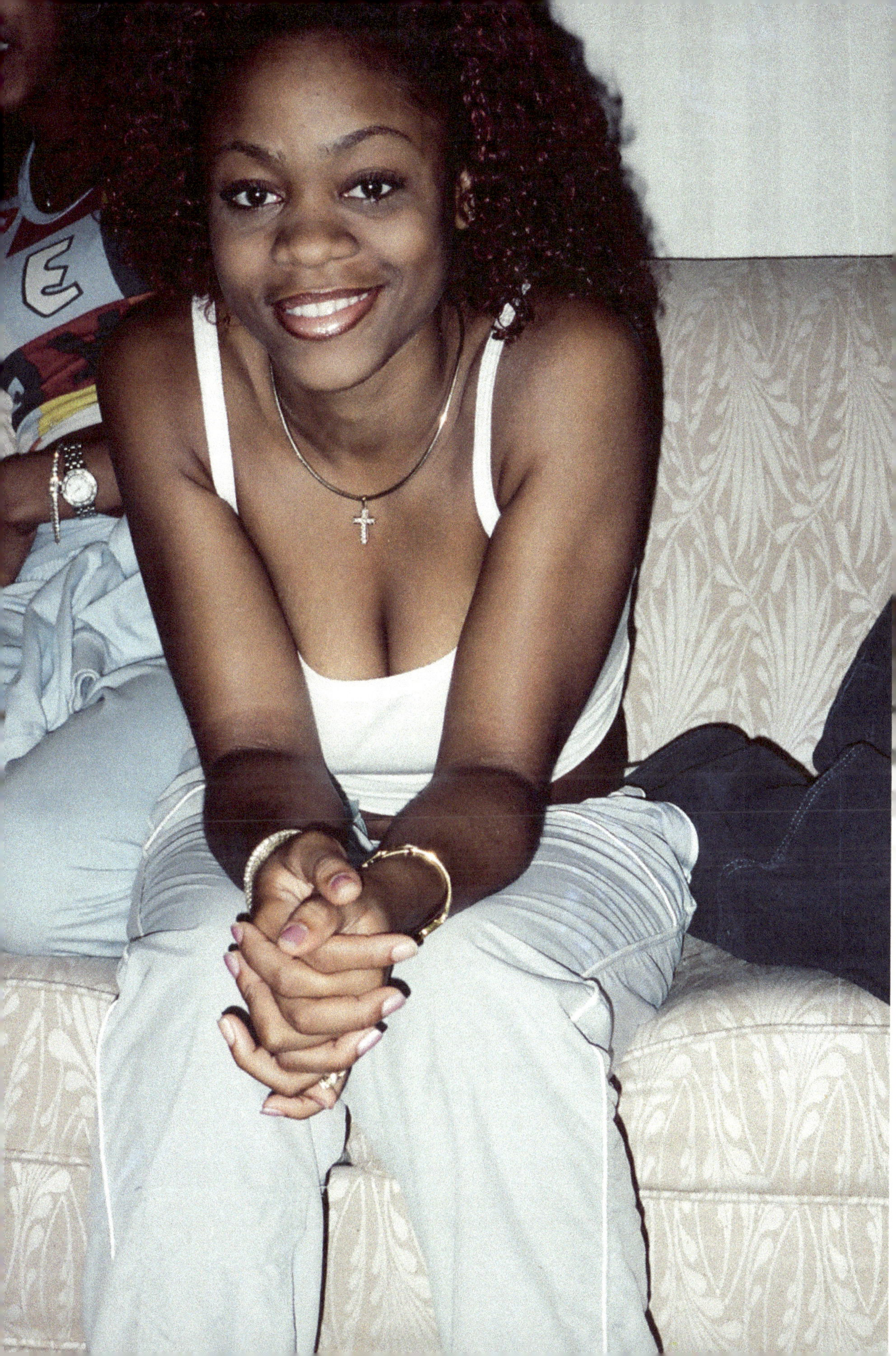

Beyoncé Knowles:

Right. So they'll be like 'Oh man, I've just spent my last dime.' Want you to be 'Oh, well then I'll get it.'

LaTavia Roberson:

I'd be like "We won't eat, sorry."

Beyoncé Knowles:

But say for instance our first single, "Bills". I think a lot of guys if they do hear it, they're only going to listen to the chorus, which is "Can you pay my bills? Can you pay my telephone bill?" And they gonna go, 'Oh, Destiny's Child some gold-diggers!' But that's not true. What am I trying to say? The verses are it's about a relationship that takes place, and the guy's treating the girl well, really well. Not necessarily having to spend money on her but taking her to places.

LeToya Luckett:

Taking her places she's never seen or been before, and eventually, he starts acting a fool, like taking her car out and bringing it back on 'E'. Buying her gifts with her own money, maxing out her credit card, just trifling' stuff like that. And she asking that one guy -

Beyoncé Knowles:

One guy!

LaTavia Roberson:

Out of all the men in the world, that one guy, can you be responsible? Can you pay the bill that you run up?

Kelly Rowland:

That he's run up.

This whole thing, like TLC on "No Scrubs", why is it at the forefront now?

Beyoncé Knowles:

I think it's been...

LeToya Luckett:

I think, Whitney Houston, "It's Not Right", that was out.

Beyoncé Knowles:

It's a lot of other songs that were out, but I think its now, like a lot of women are like...

LeToya Luckett:

Stepping up to the plate, right.

Kelly Rowland:

Men had been doing it for years though.

Beyoncé Knowles:

That's for like the guys who are like 'Oh Lord, I've had enough.'

LeToya Luckett:

Men have been doing it for years though. Men have always in their songs been calling girls gold-diggers, how they don't do anything, sick of working off of them -

Kelly Rowland:

But now, but as soon as a girl says something, there's a problem.

LaTavia Roberson:

"You wanna sip Mo' on my living room flo'"

LaTavia Roberson:

Not do anything.

LaTavia Roberson:

There's nothing wrong with those songs though.

LeToya Luckett:

Right, 'cause I don't get offended 'cause I know I ain't gold-digger or dug off of nobody. I pay my bills, do my thang. They can call girls this or they call us that, but as soon as a girl call a guy a scrub they want to go cry in the corner, and that's not fair. You know what I'm saying? Because I know there's girls out there just like I know it's guy scrubs out there.

Beyoncé Knowles:

We know that there are some girls that do the same thing in a relationship but instead of guys saying it like the girls do, and like the song, and listen to it and say 'Oh yeah, girls do that and not take it personally. Not all guys but some guys are only listening to the chorus and not listening to the fact that the guy is running up the bills and that's why we're acting like that.

Kelly Rowland:

This is Kelly. That's 'cause they've got a guilty conscious. We had to write the song from a female's perspective; we couldn't write it from how a man feels about it. But that's why in all of our interviews we clear it up and say that we know that there are women out there who want men to pay their bills for no reason. And men, they've had women that come in and buy them clothes with they own credit cards and maxed out their credit cards, used that card. We know that, but we can't write about that because we're writing about how a woman would feel if it was done to her.

Beyoncé Knowles:

Because we're women.

Kelly Rowland:

We can't write it from a male perspective, so we write it the only way that we can, and we don't want the guy to take offence to it. If you like the song - like the song.

LeToya Luckett:

And take it from a male's standpoint.

Kelly Rowland:

It's not that deep for us but it was just a fun song for us to do, and we like the song and the fact that we got to write on it it's just an experience. We're not trying to put anybody down or anything if it don't apply to you.

Did Kandi and others help with lyrics?

Beyoncé Knowles:

Yes, they came up with the basic concept. We wrote the verses with her and the bridge with her.

Your voice popped up on this album, especially on "Bug A Boo".

Beyoncé Knowles:

Thank you.

Did you take any lessons?

Beyoncé Knowles:

No, just the first album we didn't have a lot of say so, and we just did what other people told us to do. On this album, we know how we sound best, so we had a lot more input because we wanted to make sure that we could sing. I mean, showcase our vocal abilities, and that's why we got involved because it don't get right. I mean, if somebody else don't know then how are they supposed to bring out the best in you? That's why we decided that we would learn as much as we could doing the first time around, so the second time we could showcase more of our vocal abilities. Even though all of us have mature vocals.

You used Next. Why Next? There are a million groups to use. Why them?

LaTavia Roberson:

We went on tour with them.

Beyoncé Knowles:

Also, we figured that would be a wonderful duet to do with them because Next is one of the hottest guy groups out and we're cool with them, and we love their style, so we decided to hook it up with them again because they were cool.

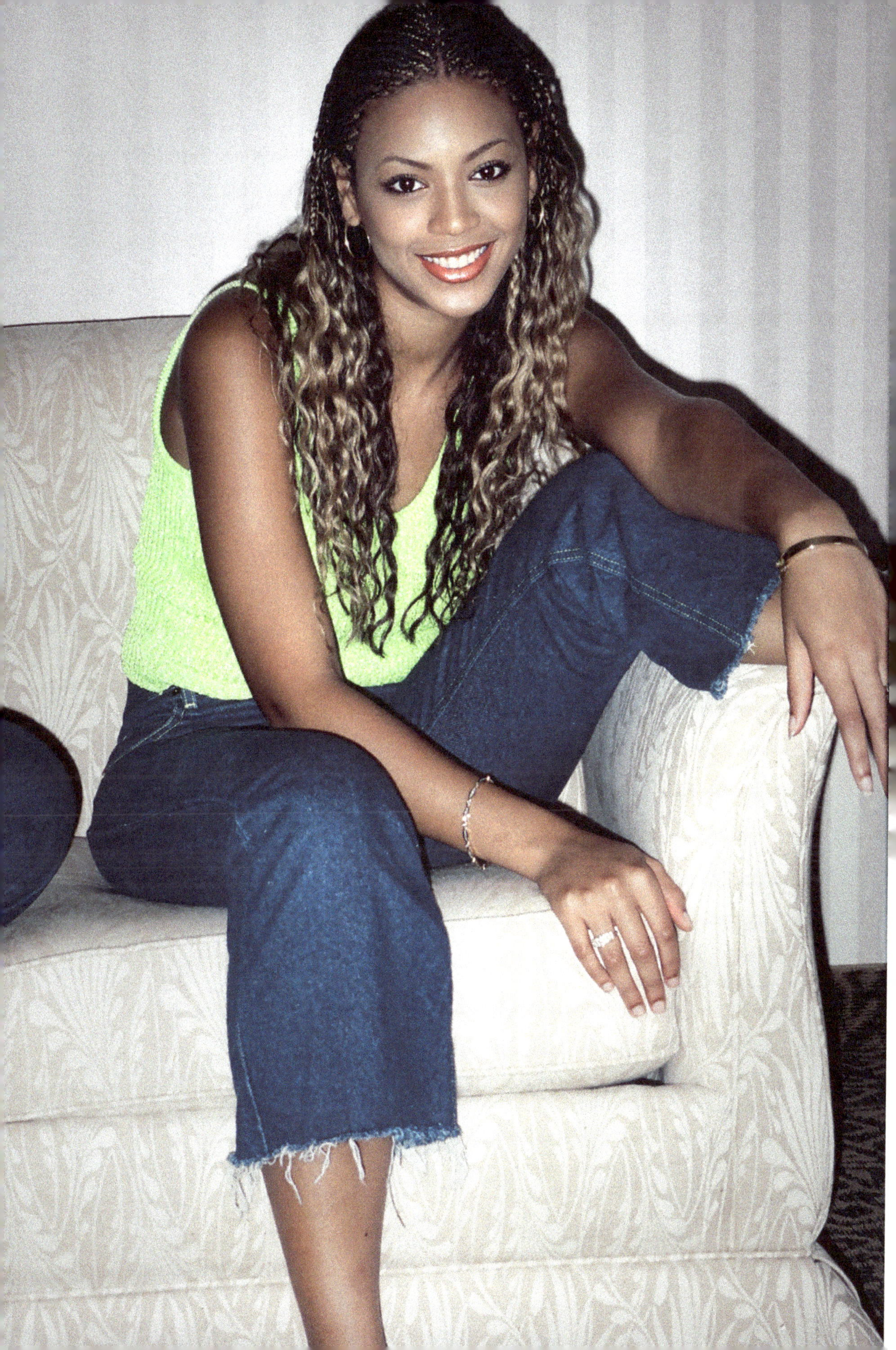

LeToya Luckett:

They said they wanted to do it on the tour, so we decided we gonna eventually make that happen, and we did.

Kelly Rowland:

We had been on tour with them for months. So we had known them, and it's like we're all cool, and they were hot, and they were we want to do a song with y'all and we were we want to do a song with y'all. It was easy.

How do you keep on top of your business? Is everything straight? Are you happy with Sony?

Beyoncé Knowles:

Yeah, I think we just... Our Manager has always taught us since we were 9 and 10 to always take business seriously, and always look out on whatever is happening around you, and always be alert and look at everything that's taking place.

LaTavia Roberson:

If you got a question, ask. If you ever want to know something we can ask it.

What do you want to put out there that hasn't got out there about you before?

Beyoncé Knowles:

We basically - I mean, what do you mean? What message do you mean?

Anything. Whatever's clever. What do you want people to know about you?

LaTavia Roberson:

We want everybody to know that we can sing and our album is hot.

LeToya Luckett:

And we want you to go pick it up.

Beyoncé Knowles:

And we want everybody to pick it up.

LeToya Luckett:

And we want to be taken seriously.

Kelly Rowland:

Right, that was what I was about to say. I think that we want more respect as a female group in this business.

Beyoncé Knowles:

Because people look at us and our age -

Kelly Rowland:

They're like 'Oh, you're young.'

Beyoncé Knowles:

But it's not -

LaTavia Roberson:

We got something to say too.

Beyoncé Knowles:

We got something to put out, and we want people to take us seriously, and to know that this album is a lot different from the first, and it moved up three notches, and we need everybody to pick it up. We need everybody's support.

Right now you got "Bills, Bills, Bills." What's the next single?

Beyoncé Knowles and LaTavia Roberson:

We're not sure.

Beyoncé Knowles:

Everybody has different favourite songs. Like probably -

LeToya Luckett:

It's "Bug A Boo", then it's "Say My Name", then it's "So Good". So, we don't know.

Kelly Rowland:

We might do like a poem on the Internet or something and see what the majority of America says that they think it should be....

Beyoncé Knowles:

The internet is www....

Kelly Rowland:

Yeah, they can write into our new website-

LeToya Luckett and Kelly Rowland:

www.dc-unplugged.com.

Kelly Rowland:

So, they can always write it in. You can see it's like styling tips that we give, there's pictures of us now and then, it's nice.

Beyoncé Knowles:

You don't want to see the then pictures.

Kelly Rowland:

It's different than our first website. It's really-

Beyoncé Knowles:

It's a lot more-

Kelly Rowland:

Nice.

Beyoncé Knowles:

Yeah, it's a lot like, it has a lot of like-I know what impressed me about the new website is that it's so colourful and there's so much more information.

Kelly Rowland:

Yeah, you can hear the album on there and everything.

Beyoncé Knowles:

It's good.

You keep saying that you were not taken seriously the first time around.

LaTavia Roberson:

No. It's not that we weren't taken seriously, it's because of our age. They look at us they're like 'Oh, they're little girls.' They're like- Because I know a lot of times we will get the question 'What do y'all know about love? Y'all only 16.'

Beyoncé Knowles:

Or what do y'all know... Recently, okay, we're 18 years old. Recently, we had the question "What do y'all know about bills?"

LaTavia Roberson:

"How can y'all have a relationship?" We're 18 now. I mean...

LeToya Luckett:

We pay taxes now, and there are bills.

LaTavia Roberson:

Everything that we name; automobiles, all of those credit card bills, we all have them.

LeToya Luckett:

Yes, we do.

Beyoncé Knowles:

I mean, I think that people took us, but I think people didn't know our abilities. I mean, they didn't know our vocal abilities because not enough people heard the album. That's why we're hoping that more people will get this album. July 27th, **The Writing's On The Wall.**

What did the first one do, two million?

LaTavia Roberson:

No. The single did.

Beyoncé Knowles:

Well, the album did a million.

Kelly Rowland:

Worldwide we sold over a million albums.

Beyoncé Knowles:

But just in America, it was Gold.

LaTavia Roberson:

A little over Gold.

Kelly Rowland:

It did 700 000. I heard 830, but I don't know. But the single, it sold over 2 million.

I read about your European success. Why are you going over so well there?

Beyoncé Knowles:

They like "Get On The Bus".

LaTavia Roberson:

I think they like our music a lot. They like "Get On The Bus".

Kelly Rowland:

"Get On The Bus", the first week on the charts it was like number 8.

Beyoncé Knowles:

But that was a surprise to us because over here it did ok. What's so wonderful to me about European fans is that people over in the States are very, but they're like even more open-minded because things are so advanced sort of over there, and they're a lot more loyal. Once you give them something that they love they'll stick with you like forever.

Kelly Rowland:

Once they love you, they love you. They don't say 'Oh well, I'm not feeling Destiny's Child that much on this song.'

LeToya Luckett:

I'm gonna wait until they come out with something I like.

Kelly Rowland:

'I'm gonna wait until they come out with something tight soon, again.' It's just like, once they like you, they like you. You feel appreciated when people appreciate your work like that. But the European success was a surprise; it was a surprise.

Beyoncé Knowles:

When they told us that we were number 8 the first week on the charts over there for "Get On The Bus" we were like 'What?' Because we didn't see it like a popping single in the States. But when they told us about the European success, and everything else that happened with "No, No, No" and the album and everything, we were just like 'What?' And then we went over there, and we recently did a tour there, 18 days in December, and that was a big success because we got a big crowd every night and it was always just energetic, and we were excited to be there every night. So it was a lot of fun, and we were blessed to have that success that we have over in Europe.

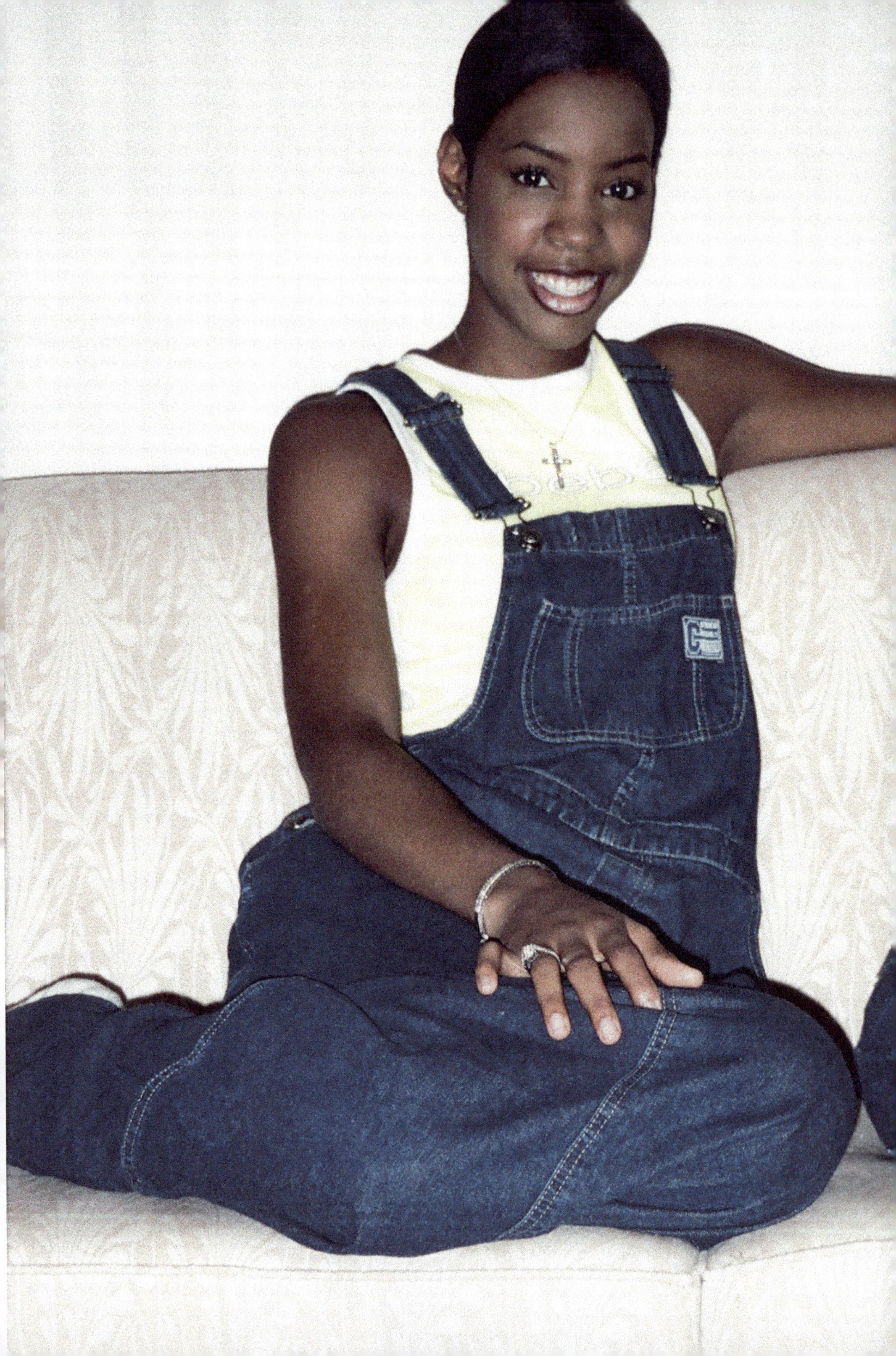

Where does Houston fit into everything?

Beyoncé Knowles:

We're not really in Houston a lot, as much as we would like to be, but when we're at home, they're supportive. We were the first female R&B group to ever come out of Houston, so it was kind of hard to get started out of Houston because it wasn't something that...

LeToya Luckett:

It's not L.A. or New York.

Beyoncé Knowles:

A lot of Rap artists and H-Town had came up. They were the first groups. And Terry from En Vogue was a member, and there was a lot of other people, but we were the first R&B group to ever come out. And then we were so young, so people they were like 'How can you guys pull this off?' But we did. And now they show us a lot of love. It's nice because we can still walk around the mall and stuff. People will say 'Heyyy!' but they're so used to us because they've been seeing us performing around Houston since we were nine and they don't really trip, not trip, but they don't really like ask for autographs anymore. They say Hi.

Is there a Houston mindset that you put across on the albums?

LaTavia Roberson:

Mindset?

Houston flavour?

LeToya Luckett:

I think our album does have a Southern flavour to it.

Kelly Rowland:

I think the music is starting to come...

Beyoncé Knowles:

I did a song with Chad Elliot on the album that the sound is Southern.

LaTavia Roberson:

Kind of Juvenile-ish.

Beyoncé Knowles:

We have some Southern stuff called "Jumpin' Jumpin" representing the South.

Correct me if I'm wrong. Are you singing from a male perspective on certain songs?

LaTavia Roberson:

We can be.

Beyoncé Knowles:

Both.

LeToya Luckett:

Some of the songs are unisex.

Kelly Rowland:

Some of the songs aren't talking from experience; we're just saying.

A 3rd person?

LaTavia Roberson:

Like "Stay" is definitely from a female perspective. All the way....

LaToya Luckett:

I mean it can be ... because dudes could be waiting too.

Beyoncé Knowles:

"Jumpin'" is talking about ladies and men. In the beginning, the first verse is dedicated to the ladies. The 2nd verse is dedicated to the men, so it's about the majority of them. "So good" is talking ... anybody can relate.

LeToya Luckett:

Teachers, co-workers, social workers.

LaTavia Roberson:

Everybody can relate.

The album is extremely personal.

Beyoncé Knowles:

Yes, it's like a conversation, but everybody can make it their kind of personal thing, it can be. I mean, the whole album is just like a slumber party because it's sort of like what girls talk about.

Kelly Rowland:

I know that when I listen to an album that sounds very personal, for example, Kelly Price's album. I think that it's so personal and I can relate to almost every song on her album, and I think when I know that that could have happened it makes me feel it so much more, my God. You could tell it by the way she is singing, that woman was hurt, or that has happened to her before, or she knows somebody that that happened to.

LeToya Luckett:

Ohhhhh! Toni Braxton! *Secrets* album!

Kelly Rowland:

There's so many women, so many that I was using that as an example right off the top of my head. I think when people know that it's personal, and by telling them that it's personal from us, I think people can feel stuff a lot more when they know that it's true. They're not just writing it for fun or leisure or whatever.

Tell me about your production. What are you doing?

Beyoncé Knowles:

I don't produce the tracks. I produce the vocals and do the vocal arrangements, and delegate the lyrics along with whoever is the writer, who writes the lyrics. The producing job is to bring out the best in the artist when they're producing vocals and to put everything together, put the whole song together. That's what I got a chance to do on a lot of the songs.

Give me some background. Did you start when you were nine years old, and you've been friends since time?

LaTavia Roberson:

Since we've been in elementary school.

LeToya Luckett:

Yeah, just like in the bio, the same thing. Did you get the first bio or the second bio?

The new one.

LeToya Luckett:

The new one? It is not in there, but we got started like eight years ago, eight or nine years ago.... nine years ago!

Beyoncé Knowles:

1990.

Kelly Rowland:

We got started nine years ago, and we all met each other in elementary school. Beyoncé brought LeToya to the group. LaTavia brought me to the group, and we've just been performing and being together and becoming sisters and growing up in the music industry together.

LeToya Luckett:

All together.

Is there a leader?

Beyoncé Knowles:

A leader? I mean, we all... I sing lead. Kelly sings second lead. LaTavia sings alto. LeToya sings soprano.

LeToya Luckett:

Are you talking about personality wise?

Beyoncé Knowles:

We each have different traits about us. I'm serious, and I'm like the mother of the group. I'm like the one that's gonna say 'Alright y'all, we need to do this and we need to do that.' Kelly is sensitive. Kelly is the 'Why can't we all just get along?' type. And LaTavia is the sassy one. She's the real one that's going to break it down and be real. And LeToya is the one that if everything goes tight, or says something, she's also the 'Why can't we all just get along?' But in a happier, in a joking way. You know how if you're serious and tired just like somebody there that is gonna make a joke to make everything better, that's LeToya.

Kelly Rowland:

When there's too much stress, LeToya always says break that, break that.

Beyoncé Knowles:

So when you put it all together, it's a good combination, and that's how we've gotten the chance to deal with each other and work together for so long.

Do you ever get into any fights or arguments?

LaTavia Roberson:

Girl fights. Not no cat fights or nothing. Not no-

Beyoncé Knowles:

It's like your sister. We're just like sisters. Sisters get into arguments, but eventually, they talk about things. I mean, it's like our love is deeper than this group and it's deeper than an argument. You might be mad for a day or two, but we get over it.

LeToya Luckett:

We talk about it.

Beyoncé Knowles:

Communication is the key.

Anything else?

LeToya Luckett:

We'd like to thank everybody for supporting us on our first album and for making it go platinum internationally and to support us on the second album, which comes out July 27.

Beyoncé Knowles:

And the single "Bills, Bills, Bills" will be in stores June 15.

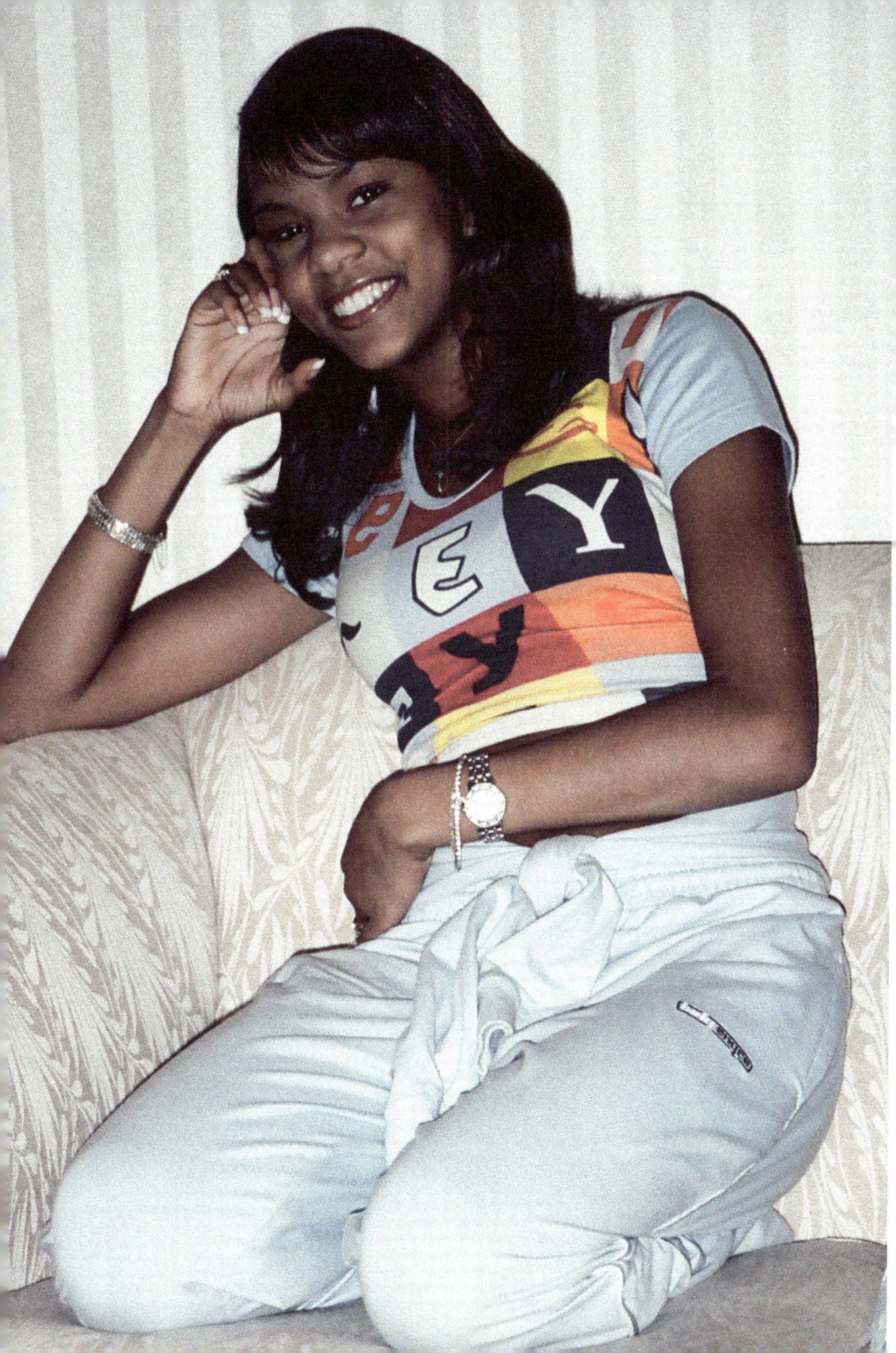

LeToya Luckett:

And check out our website www.dc-unplugged.com. That's the first time I said that and got it right!

Beyoncé Knowles:

And thank God for that because we're not Destiny's Child without him, and we also love Canada, and that was the first place we ever got a plaque.

LaTavia Roberson:

My favourite place is Vancouver.

LeToya Luckett:

Mine is hanging up in my house. I love Vancouver.

This is coming out June 25th- You're coming July 24th to Canada, to Toronto.

Beyoncé Knowles:

Oh really? Didn't know that.

Kelly Rowland:

No, we didn't. You know how long we're going to be there? Are we doing different parts of Canada?

I read that you're playing a theme park.

Kelly Rowland:

Oh, that's fun.

Maybe you can go in front of the rides.

Beyoncé Knowles:

Oh, we got a chance to do that. We always dreamed of that since we were like little wee when we all used to go to *AstroWorld*.

LeToya Luckett:

And be like 'One day! One day! We're gonna get to go to the front of the line.' And we finally- Just recently we did a photoshoot in Six Flags, and they took us to the front of the line. And now, I know...

Beyoncé Knowles:

And we got to ride the rides like two or three times.

LaTavia Roberson:

And everybody was getting mad.

LeToya Luckett:

People in the line were looking at us like 'Who the hell... Who are they?' And we like "I'm sorry y'all."

Beyoncé Knowles:

They were trying to take pictures while we were on the ride.

Kelly Rowland:

Yeah, we had to go on rides like five times. Our stomachs was just like-

Beyoncé Knowles:

Yeah, we had to go upside down a couple of times, and it was a little-

LeToya Luckett:

Hectic.

Cool. I want to get some shots, casual shots.

Destiny's Child:

Ohhhhhhhhhhhhhhhhhh!!!!

Beyoncé Knowles:

No. No.

Kelly Rowland:

We weren't told at all.

Beyoncé Knowles:

We could put on some makeup real quick.

Okay. How long is that going to take?

Beyoncé Knowles:

Like ten minutes?

LaTavia Roberson:

Do I look like a ten-minute face right now? Uh-uh.

Beyoncé Knowles:

You got to put on a little powder.

I need casual shots.

Beyoncé Knowles:

He don't want it to look like we made up. He wants it to look like we look like.

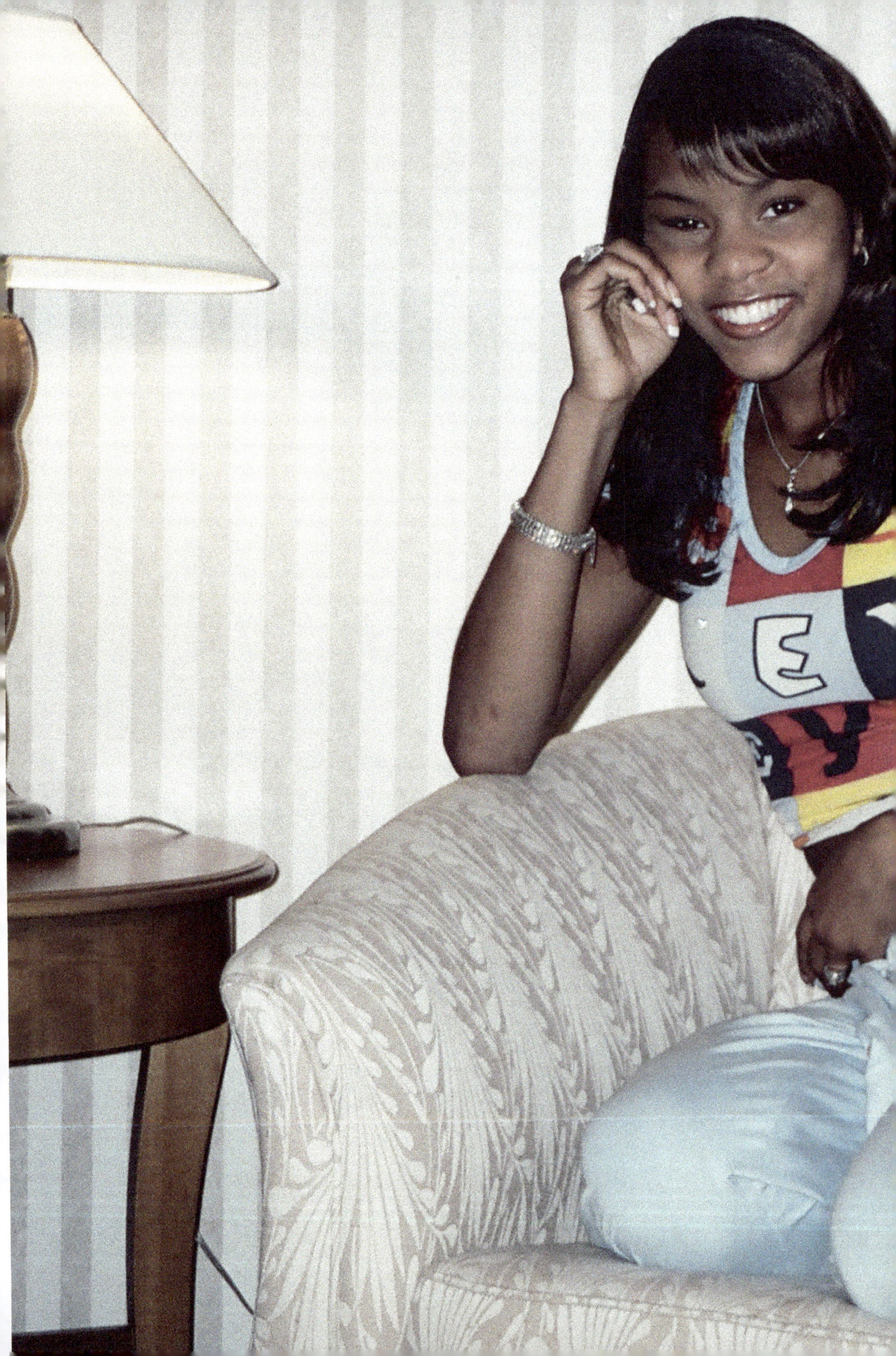

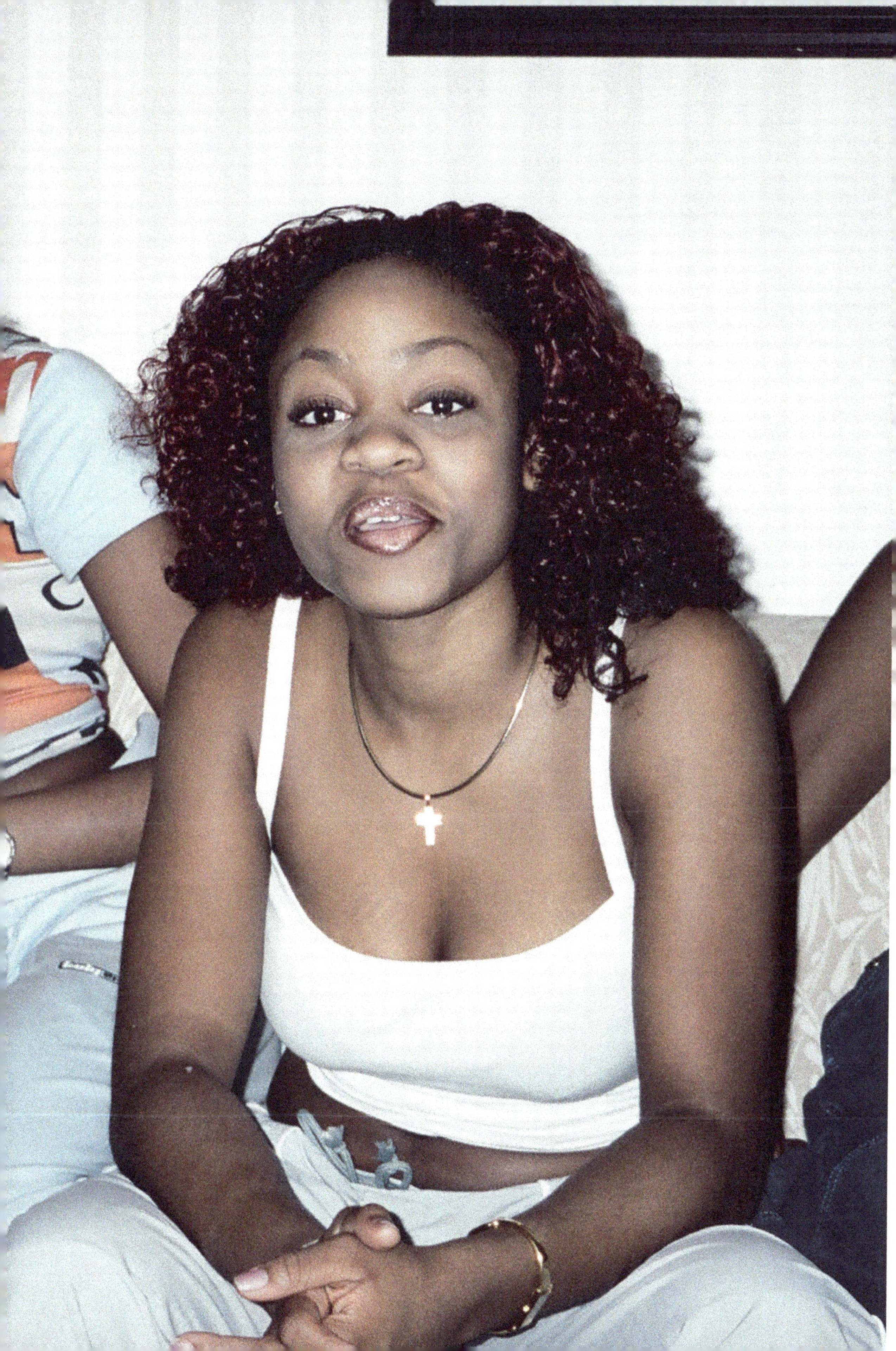

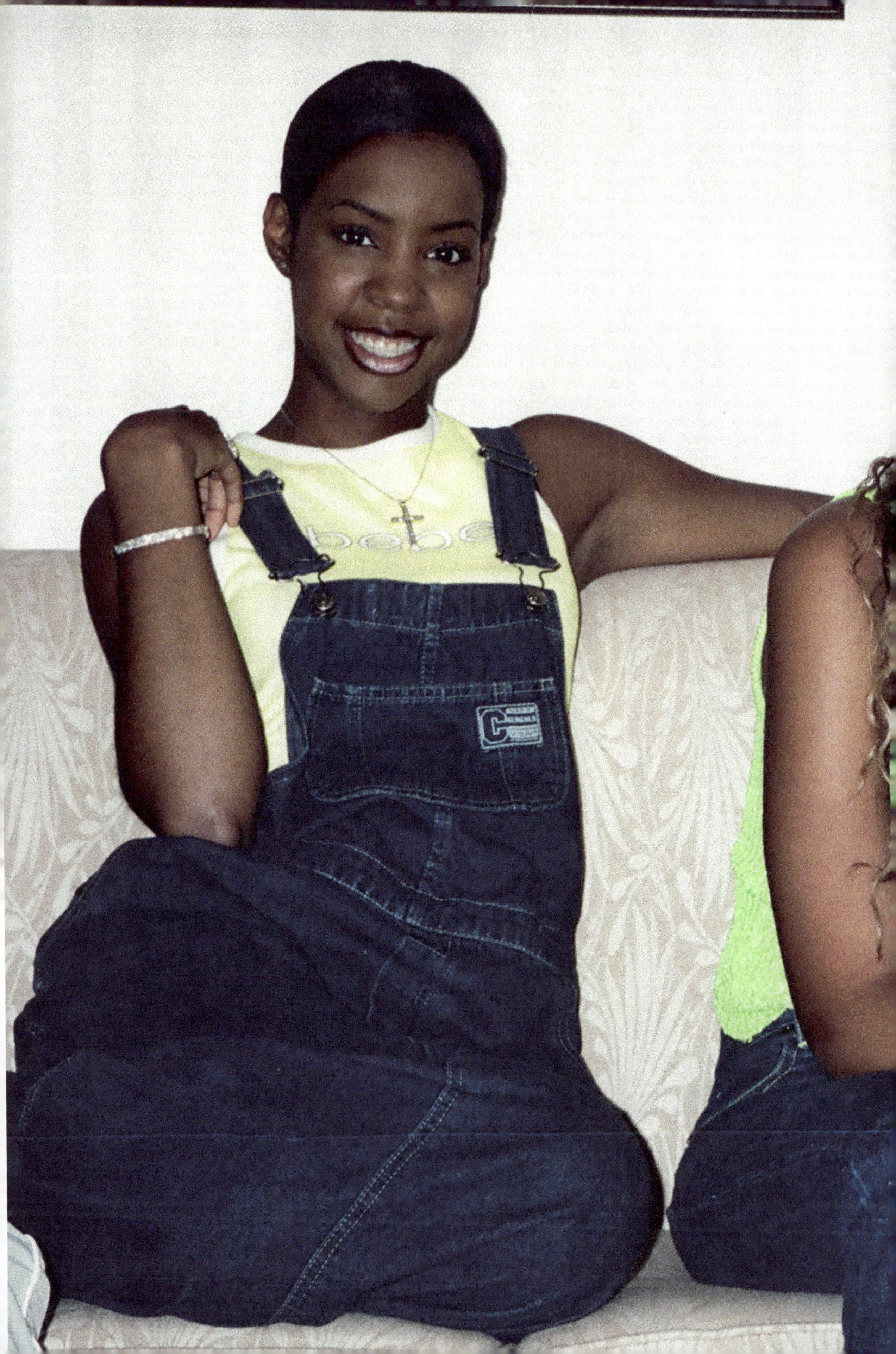

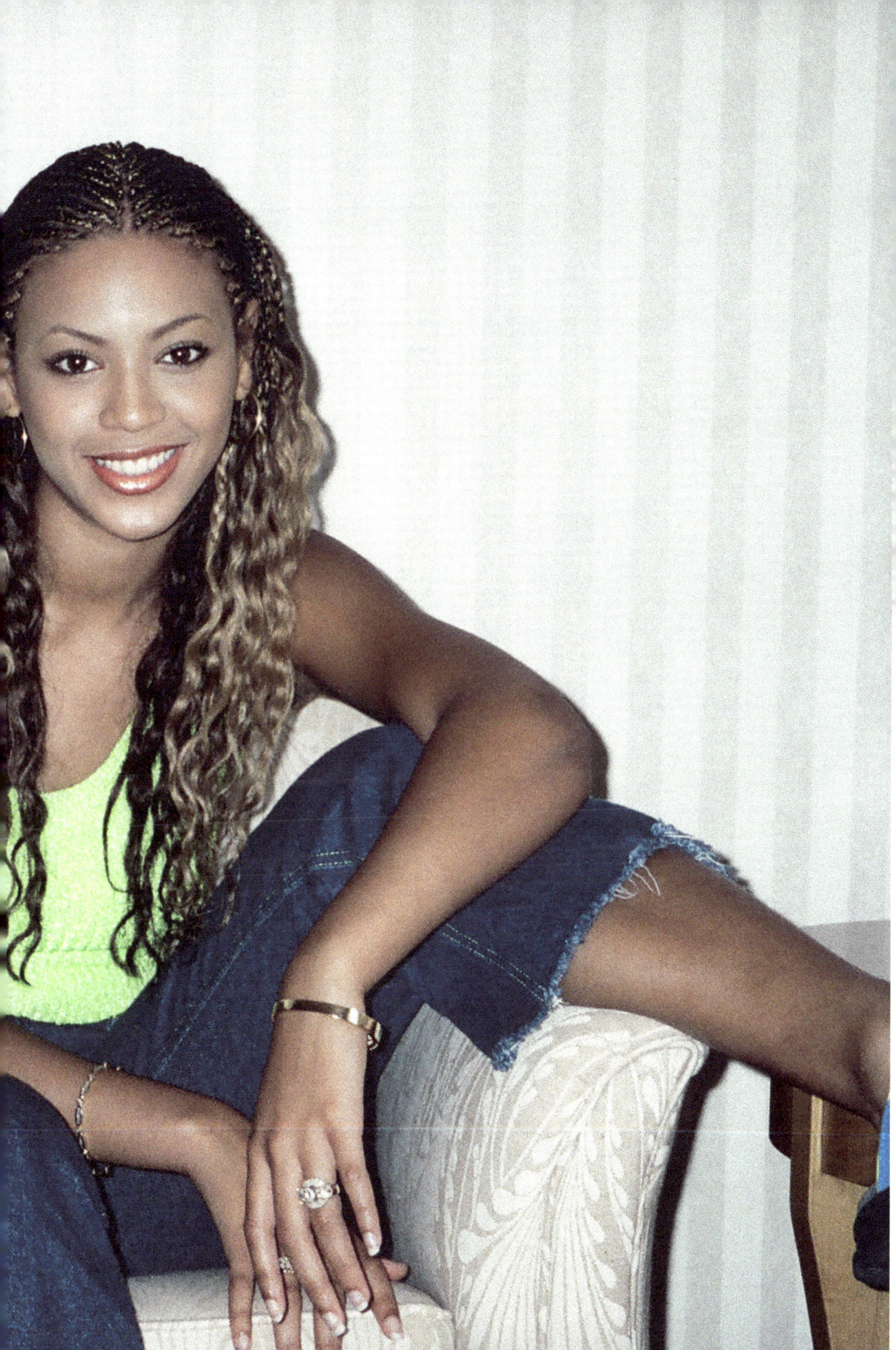

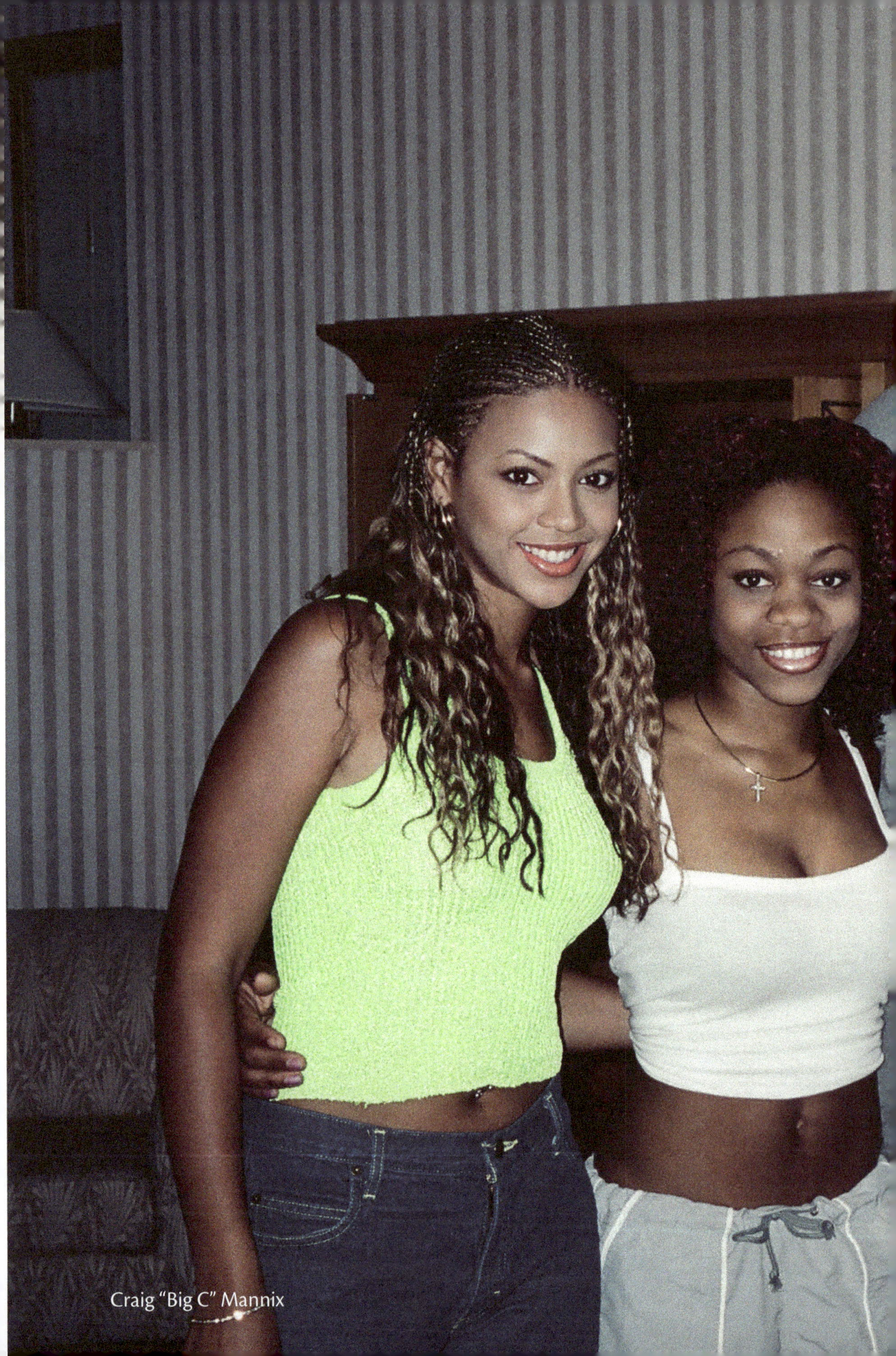

Craig "Big C" Mannix

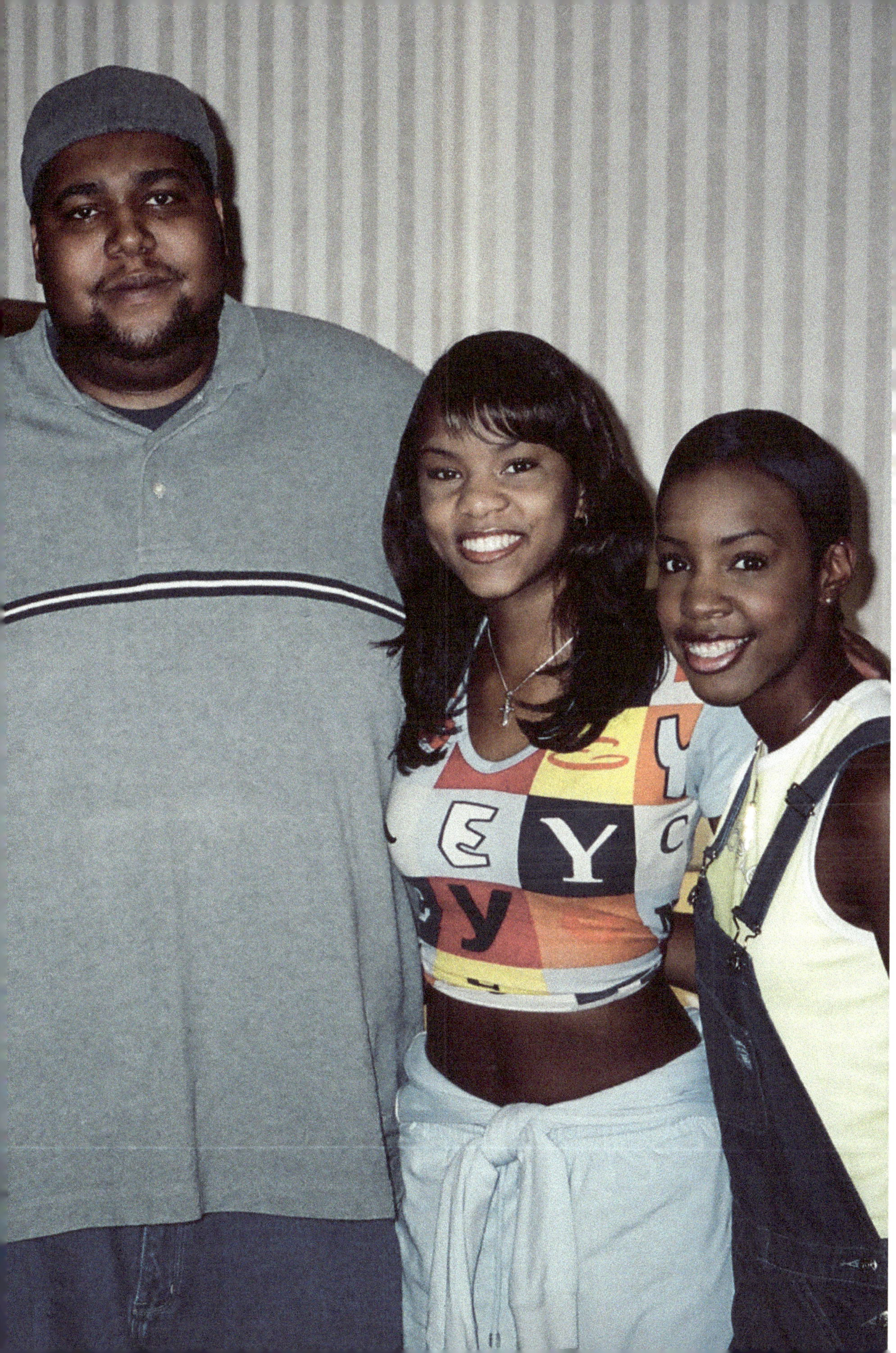

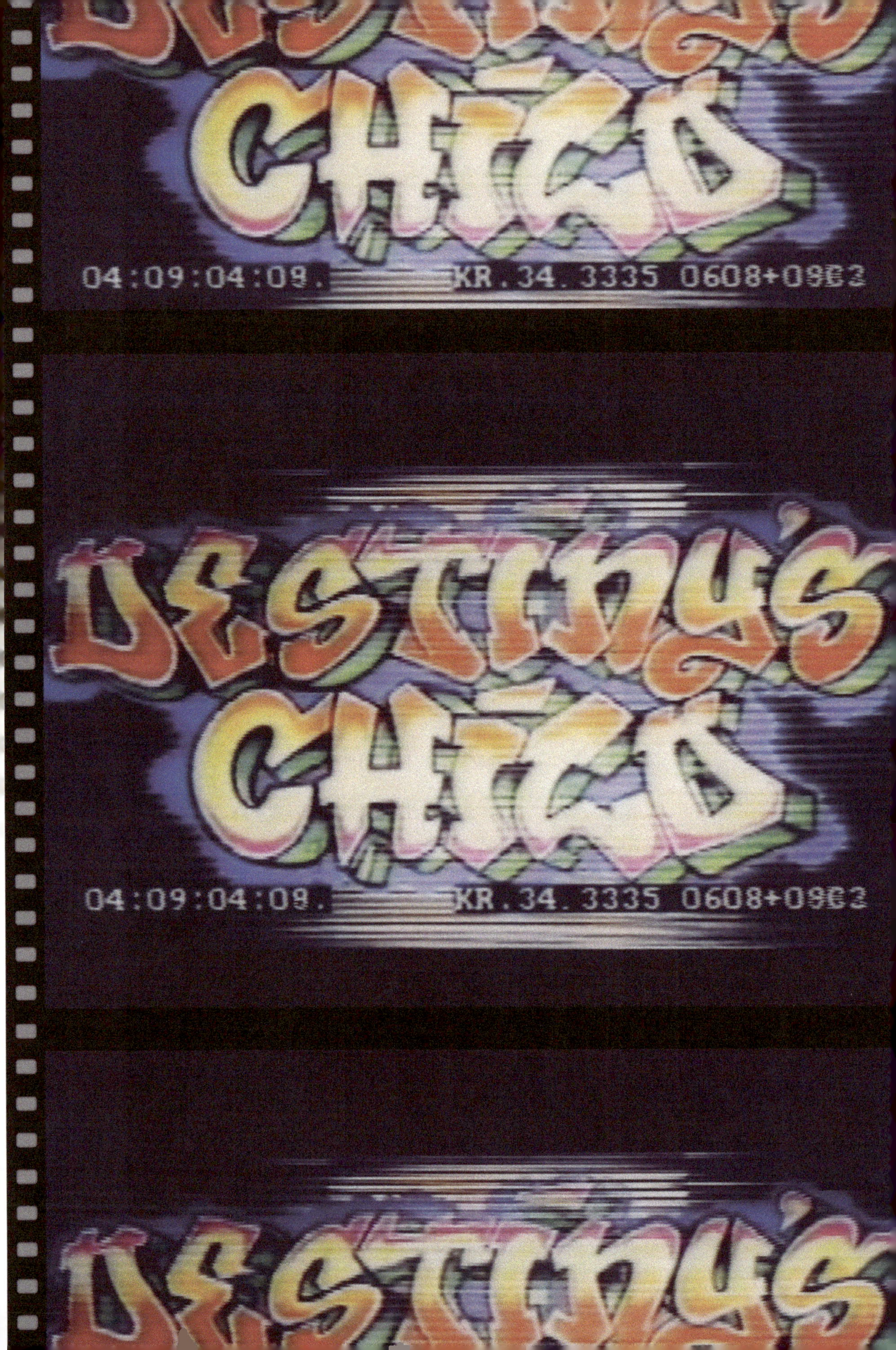

DESTINY'S CHILD
04:09:04:09.   KR.34.3335 0608+0963

DESTINY'S CHILD
04:09:04:09.   KR.34.3335 0608+0963

THE WRITING'S ON THE WALL

AN EXCLUSIVE SONG-BY-SONG BREAKDOWN BY BEYONCÉ KNOWLES, KELLY ROWLAND, LATAVIA ROBERSON AND LETOYA LUCKETT

Destiny's Child participated in a song-by-song breakdown of *The Writing's On The Wall.* It is a both a compelling look into the creative thought process behind the album and what consumed them individually and collectively at the time.

The group were skillfully guided step-by-step through the entire process of creating their debut album. *The Writing's On The Wall* sessions had provided an opportunity to project themselves into the songs, and they jumped at the chance to feature their vocal abilities. Destiny's Child discussed their writing and production contributions to the album, the inspiration behind the lyrical ideas and the song-writing process. Beyoncé took a special interest in the vocal production and arrangements.

LeToya Luckett:

OK, "The Intro". This is LeToya. And how we got it together was Kandi Burruss from Xscape came up with the concept, with The Godfather thing. So we went in the studio, like some fools, put tissue in our mouth and everything. We watched the movie first and then watched the *Set It Off-*

Beyoncé Knowles:

We watched *The Godfather*.

LeToya Luckett:

I said the movie. We watched the movie and then we did the *Set It Off* movie. You know when they're sitting around the table, and they have grapes in their mouth. We was like let's do that concept and so we just went in the studio and kind of did a summary of the album using *The Godfather* technique.

Kelly Rowland:

Song number two, "So Good", is about how everybody put us down. They were like 'Y'all will never make it' or whatever and everything, and they smile in our face now. We just saying that by the grace of God we're doing good. He helped us out, and we're grateful for what success that we've had, and we want people that hated on us to know that we're doing good. God helped us out.

Beyoncé Knowles:

We explained "Bills", so I'll explain "Bug A Boo". "Bug A Boo" is... I think that it can be a friend, a neighbour, a brother, a sister, or whatever.

LaTavia Roberson:

Girl or guy.

Beyoncé Knowles:

Yeah. A "Bug A Boo" is just somebody that bugs you. Always bugging you, calling you every 5 minutes. You can have ten voicemail messages on your voicemail, and it can all be the same person. They kind of like a friendly stalker. That's what I'm gonna call a "Bug A Boo", just a friendly stalker.

La Tavia Roberson:

"Confessions" is about a guy and a girl. They were in a relationship, and they separated, and during the time they did some things, and they think that in order for the relationship to work they know they're going to hear what each other do when they broke up. So, before they get together, they want to confess and say everything that they do, that they did when they weren't together.

LeToya Luckett:

OK, "Temptations". Everyone goes through this. We CO-wrote on this. D'wayne Wiggins did the track. But, "Temptations" is about a girl that's in a club and she has a man at home, but she sees this cutie in the corner, and she wants him. I guess some way he walks over to her, or she walks over to him, and he gives her his number, and she writes it on the palm of her hand or whatever, and then she's like 'Oops, I forgot. I got a man, and he's waiting at home.' So she's staying true to her man, but she's letting him know that it's all about being tempted. But she's staying true to who she's with.

Kelly Rowland:

OK, "Now That's She's Gone", produced by Ken Fambro. It's about a guy who used to take- Y'all were in a relationship, and he used to take you places and he like left you alone for this other girl. I guess she used him or whatever, and she left him, and now he wants to come back into your life thinking that y'all can just hit it off like then.

You like 'Boy, you ain't got it like that, to where you can keep coming back and forth to me like that. You like now that she gone you want to come back. You think you got it like that. You waited too long, so now I'm leaving you alone. I'm not messing with you anymore.

Beyoncé Knowles:

"Where'd You Go". "Where'd You Go" is about a relationship, and everything's going cool or whatever, but all of a sudden this guy he's like leaving you hanging. You don't get a call, you don't hear from him, and you ask him where are you? It's been five days! I haven't heard from you; you haven't called me, you haven't sent me a letter! Just get your friend to call me or do something. But, I mean, you just lost, and you want to know where he is, and you ask him where'd you go? Because-

Kelly Rowland:

You're worried about him if he's okay-

Beyoncé Knowles:

You're at home buggin', and you're just worried, and you ask him where'd you go?

LaTavia Roberson:

"Hey, Ladies". This song happens a lot with females. It's just saying- It's like a women's anthem. Why is it? I mean, let me start over. Ladies a lot of times fall in love, and they know that they're in a relationship and the relationship isn't right. But they are so much in love that they can't see it, and even though they do see it, they don't want to get out of the relationship because they love the guy so much. And it's just saying that ladies why do we stay in a relationship when we know it's time to go.

LeToya Luckett:

I knew I was going to get this song. I knew I was gonna get this song, which is "If You Leave" featuring Next. This song is like a 90's "Secret Lovers". Remember that song?

Beyoncé Knowles:

No, no, no.

LeToya Luckett:

Yes, it is! 'Cause they both... Let me tell you why. Because in that song they both-

Beyoncé Knowles:

Explain the song.

LeToya Luckett:

Right, but- Well, you know the subject of that song and how they both- She got a man- I mean, she got a man, and he got a woman, but they want to be together. I guess because their other person's - The relationships they're in right now aren't working. So, they want to get out of it and run away and be together.

It's like the girl, her guy has cheated on her but with her best friend, such is life, and the guy, she and the guy, well, RL in this situation. His girlfriend has wrecked his car, slept with his best friend, does some unnecessary stuff, and they both had that same thing happen, so they want to run away together.

Beyoncé Knowles:

It reminds me of like kindergarten 'cause it's like 'You leave her, I'll leave him.' Like, you pack your bags, I'll go pack mine, and we can run away together.

"Jumpin', Jumpin'", this is by Beyoncé. It's like a party song. It's about going to the club. It's like ladies, leave your men at home, you going to the club to party with the ballers, and then it's like guys, leave your girls at home, you going to the club to see all the chiquitas there that's gonna be dancing and all that stuff. So, it's about going to the club without your spouse or your boyfriend or girlfriend, and to get a party on and have fun by yourself.

Kelly Rowland:

"Say My Name"! "Say My Name"! That song, I know it's all of one of our favourites. It's just about a guy, and you call him and whatever, and he's like answering you with one-word answers, and you like 'You know, what's up, what's the deal? How come you can't just call me baby?' Usually any other day you'd be like 'How you doing, baby?' 'How is your day?' But all of a sudden he's like 'How are you?' 'Oh yeah, cool, man' Trying to make it sound like he's talking to one of his boys.

LaTavia Roberson:

'What's up, man!'

LeToya Luckett:

But you like 'OK, now see any other day you say you love me...

LaTavia Roberson:

'Hey, baby.'

LeToya Luckett:

You know, 'Hey baby.' But he answering you with all these one-word answers. So you're like 'Look, if ain't nobody there say my name. Say you love me and tell me what you usually say. Call me baby.' And she's just asking him to say your name.

Beyoncé Knowles:

"She Can't Love You". This song is about a bitch. Girl- It's about a girl who sees her ex-boyfriend's girlfriend and she kind of hates on the ex-girlfriend but-

Kelly Rowland:

On the new girlfriend.

Beyoncé Knowles:

Yeah, on his ex-girlfriend new girlfriend. She doesn't like the ex-boyfriend anymore but she still is like checking out the new girlfriend, and she's just saying that 'You told me you didn't like this in a girl. Why is she everything that you didn't like? There's no way she could love you like I love you.'

LeToya Luckett:

OK, "Stay". This song is produced by Daryl Simmons, and it's about a girl. She been in this relationship, I guess they've been together for a year, and she's really in love with this guy, and she feels it's time.

Kelly Rowland:

She wants to take it to the next level.

LeToya Luckett:

Right. She wants to take it to the next level, give up the virginity, and she's like 'Dude, if I do that will you stay, will things still be the same? Are you going to run off and leave me?' She just asking him will you still love her the same after she takes it to the next level.

Beyoncé Knowles:

I bet a forty, fifty-year-old person can think that.

LaTavia Roberson:

What's that lady's name we just saw in Miami?

Beyoncé Knowles:

Betty Wright.

LeToya Luckett:

Betty Wright.

Kelly Rowland:

"Sweet Sixteen" is produced by Beyoncé and D'wayne Wiggins. It's about a girl who is 16, and she falls in love with this older guy. He's like way older than her, and he makes the obvious promises, and he gets her pregnant, and you're telling the girl 'Slow down, there's so much more in life for you out there, just slow down you're moving too fast. Just cherish your life and slow down.'

Beyoncé Knowles:

And the "Outro". We did "Amazing Grace" for Miss Andretta Tillman, and she was our Manager, CO-Manager. And she also was with us ever since the group first started, ever since we were like nine and ten, and she passed away, and like on the first album, we dedicated "My Time Has Come" to her. We just figured that it would just be right this time to dedicate "Amazing Grace" to her. She always wanted us to do a Gospel song. So we just thought it was only right, only correct to give "Amazing Grace" to Ms. Ann.

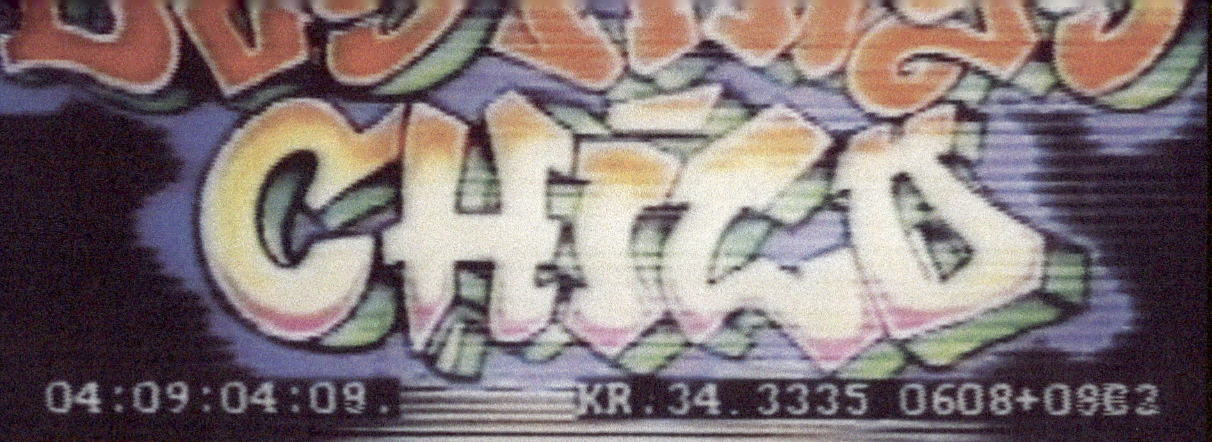

DESTINY'S CHILD
04:09:04:09.   KR.34.3335 0608+0962
DESTINY'S CHILD
04:09:04:09.   KR.34.3335 0608+0962
DESTINY'S

OUTRO

In December 1999, LaTavia Roberson and LeToya Luckett approached Destiny's Child Manager, Matthew Knowles, and discussed bringing on their own Management representation. As the father of Beyoncé, and the legal guardian and uncle of Kelly Rowland, it was perceived that they had received preferential treatment and standing within the group, along with more monies. Matthew Knowles immediately shunned them and began sourcing out new members behind the scenes.

In February 2000, LaTavia Roberson and LeToya Luckett were unceremoniously replaced without notice by Farrah Franklin and Michelle Williams. Roberson and Luckett sadly discovered their fate as the new lineup was announced by Beyoncé on **TRL** the day before the release of the "Say My Name"
video featuring Franklin and Williams. A lawsuit and nasty war of words media battle ensued.

It was alleged Mathew Knowles, Beyoncé Knowles and Kelly Rowland had breached the partnership and the legal, ethical relationship of trust, and breach of contract, defamation, libel and fraud, and damages requested. The group's label, Sony Music was also listed in the suit.

Farrah Franklin left the group on July 20, 2000, a short six months after she unveiled in the "Say My Name" video. Destiny's Child claimed she was asked to leave for lack of interest and had missed three significant dates. Franklin stated she quit due to negative vibes and her lack of decision making.

She had experienced severe dehydration and instead of being nurtured back to health by the team they berated her for not appearing in top form.

Though her time as a member of the group was limited, Farrah Franklin sang on many vital songs. Including the remixes of "Jumpin' Jumpin'", "Upside Down" (Live at VH1 Divas), "Big Momma's Theme" (**Big Momma's House** soundtrack), and "Dot".
Plus "8 Days of Christmas", "Independent Women Part I", "Independent Women Part II", "Dance With Me" and "Like Dat", cut from the **Survivor** album.

"Independent Women Part 1" was released on September 4, 2000, as the lead single for the **Charlie's Angels** soundtrack. It went straight to #1 on the Billboard Hot 100 sales chart and remained in the top spot for a record-setting 11 consecutive weeks.

Beyoncé Knowles and Kelly Rowland were dropped from the LaTavia Roberson and LeToya Luckett lawsuit in late December 2000 in exchange for an undisclosed settlement and the cessation of derogatory words by either side. Matthew Knowles still stood accused of withholding monies and abusive actions. **The Writing's On The Wall** continued to sell steady and hit 8 million copies sold.

Destiny's Child "Survivor" single released on February 13, 2001. One week later, Kelly Rowland became the first member to release a solo song on February 20, 2001, with the inclusion of "Angel" on the **Down To Earth** soundtrack. Beyoncé Knowles marked her acting debut on May 8, 2001, with the release of **Carmen: A Hip Hopera** produced for television by MTV and directed by Robert Townsend. Destiny's Child fourth #1 single, "Bootylicious" was released on May 20, 2001.

The **Survivor** album released on May 1, 2001. Beyoncé Knowles had her hands all over it, CO-producing every track and CO-writing on 14 of the 15 songs. The exception a cover of the Bee Gee's Barry and Robin Gibb penned "Emotion" originally recorded by Samantha Sang in 1978 and by the Bee Gee's in 1994.

Destiny's Child **8 Days Of Christmas** album released on October 30, 2001. The title track initially made an appearance on the UK limited edition bonus CD and European re-release of **The Writing's On The Wall.** There is also a little known Houston Edition of the album featuring a LaTavia Roberson lead vocal on "Can't Help Myself".

Destiny's Child released T**his Is The Remix** on March 12, 2002. The album included re-sung remixes of "No, No, No (Part II)", "Say My Name", "Bug A Boo", and "Emotion". The same month LaTavia Roberson and LeToya Luckett rekindled the drama and filed a federal lawsuit against Destiny's Child and Sony Music stating "Survivor" had broken their agreement by publicly disparaging them in the lyrics.

A flurry of activity followed. Michelle Williams released the first solo album of the group with her Gospel release **Heart To Yours** on April 16, 2002. Kelly Rowland released "Dilemma" with Nelly on June 25, 2002. It served as the third single from Nelly's **Nellyville** album and the lead single from Rowland's forthcoming solo album debut, **Simply Deep**. Beyoncé Knowles made her major motion picture debut on July 26, 2002, as the former lover of Austin Powers, FBI agent Foxxy Cleopatra, undercover as a Disco singer in Austin Powers in **Goldmember**.

She also contributed "Work It Out" and "Hey Goldmember" to the film soundtrack. Both LaTavia Roberson and LeToya Luckett lawsuits settled in July 2002. However, the terms were not released.

LaTavia Roberson and LeToya Luckett formed a new group called Anjel with Naty Quinones and Tiffany Beaudoin. A 22-song demo was recorded in Atlanta with Jagged Edge, and they appeared in the Jagged Edge remix video for "Where The Party At". Sadly the production company behind the project, 581 Entertainment, ceased to exist, the members sought solo projects, and the demo leaked online.

Beyoncé Knowles and her boyfriend at the time, Jay-Z, released the great statement record, "'03 Bonnie & Clyde", sampling Tupac Shakur's "Me and My Girlfriend" on October 10, 2002. Kelly Rowland's **Simply Deep** released on October 22, 2002. Behind the scenes, both Beyoncé Knowles and Kelly Rowland pursued their acting careers. Beyoncé costarred alongside Cuba Gooding, Jr. as a lounge singer in **The Fighting Temptations** while contributing music to its soundtrack. Rowland met with an ultra-violent demise towards the end of the Horror film, **Freddy vs Jason**, released on August 15, 2003.

The album the world had been waiting for finally saw the light of day on June 24, 2003, with the release of **Dangerously In Love** by Beyoncé. Michelle Williams replaced Toni Braxton in the title role of **Aida** on Broadway at the tail end of 2003 and released her second solo album, **Do You Know**, on January 26, 2004.

Destiny Fulfilled, the fourth and final Destiny's Child studio album, was released on November 15, 2004. In June 2005, the group announced that they would part ways and split up following the final North American concert dates of their **Destiny Fulfilled ... and Lovin' It Tour** in September 2005.

Destiny's Child is one of the most successful groups of all time with sales of 65 million copies worldwide. Beyoncé Knowles has sold 37 million copies as a solo artist. Kelly Rowland has sold an additional 3 million copies as a solo artist.

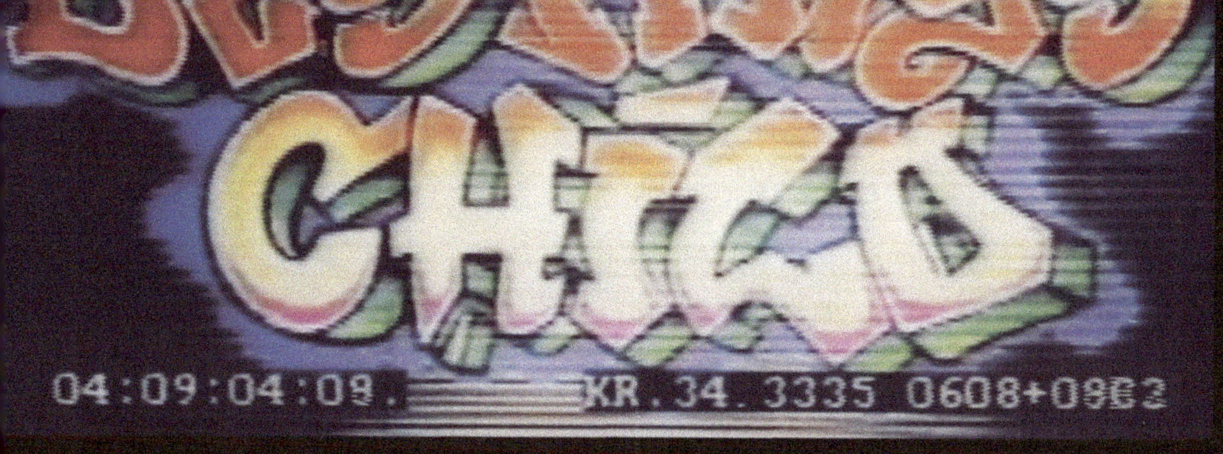
DESTINY'S
CHILD
04:09:04:09.   KR.34.3335 0608+0962

DESTINY'S
CHILD
04:09:04:09.   KR.34.3335 0608+0962

DESTINY'S

BOOTYLICIOUS REMIX VIDEO EXCLUSIVE

Exclusive images cut direct from the film of the Rockwilder "Bootylicious" Remix video featuring Missy Elliot by Director Little x, a.k.a. Director X.

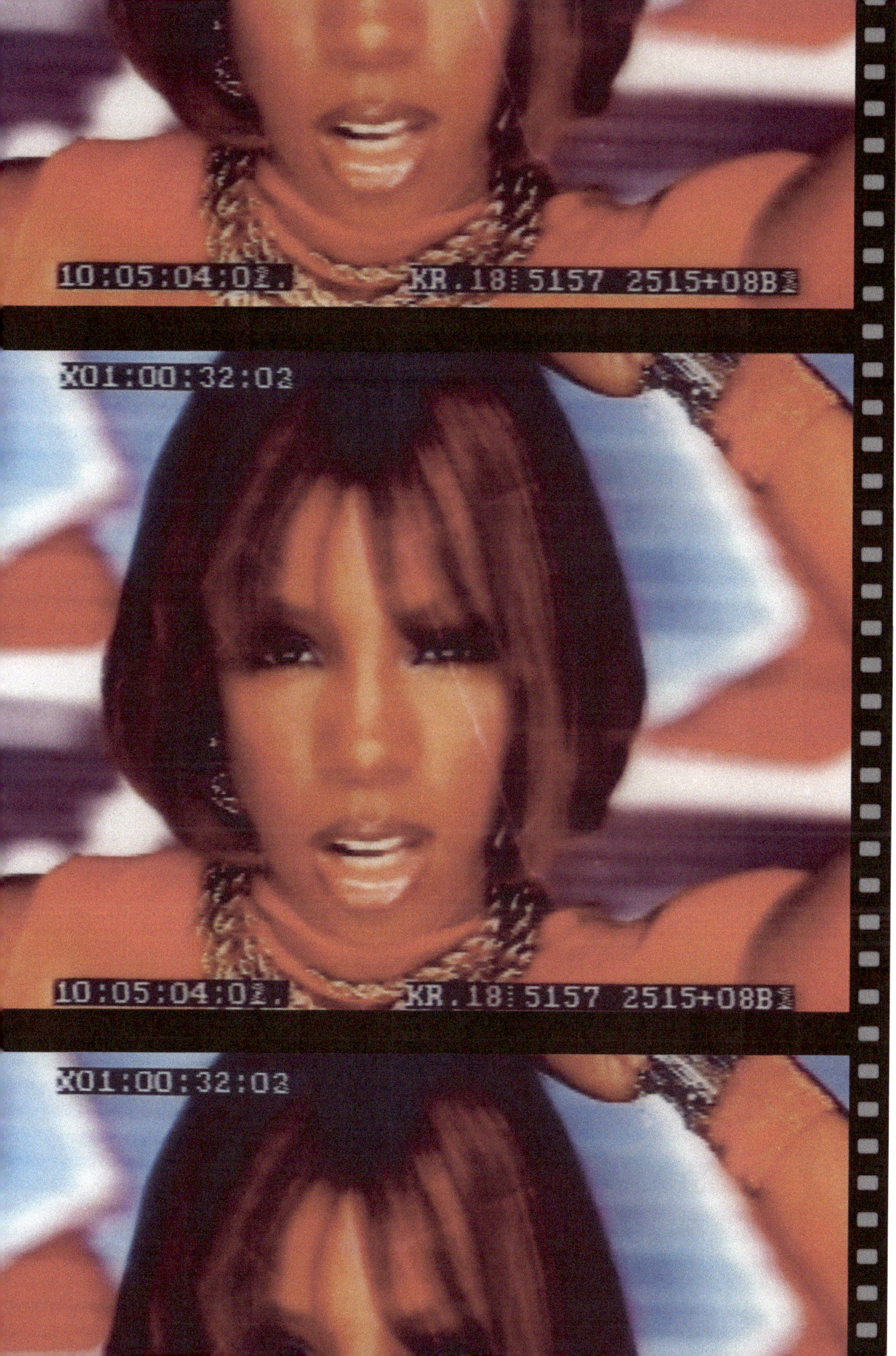
10:05:04:02. KR.18 5157 2515+08B
X01:00:32:02
10:05:04:02. KR.18 5157 2515+08B
X01:00:32:02

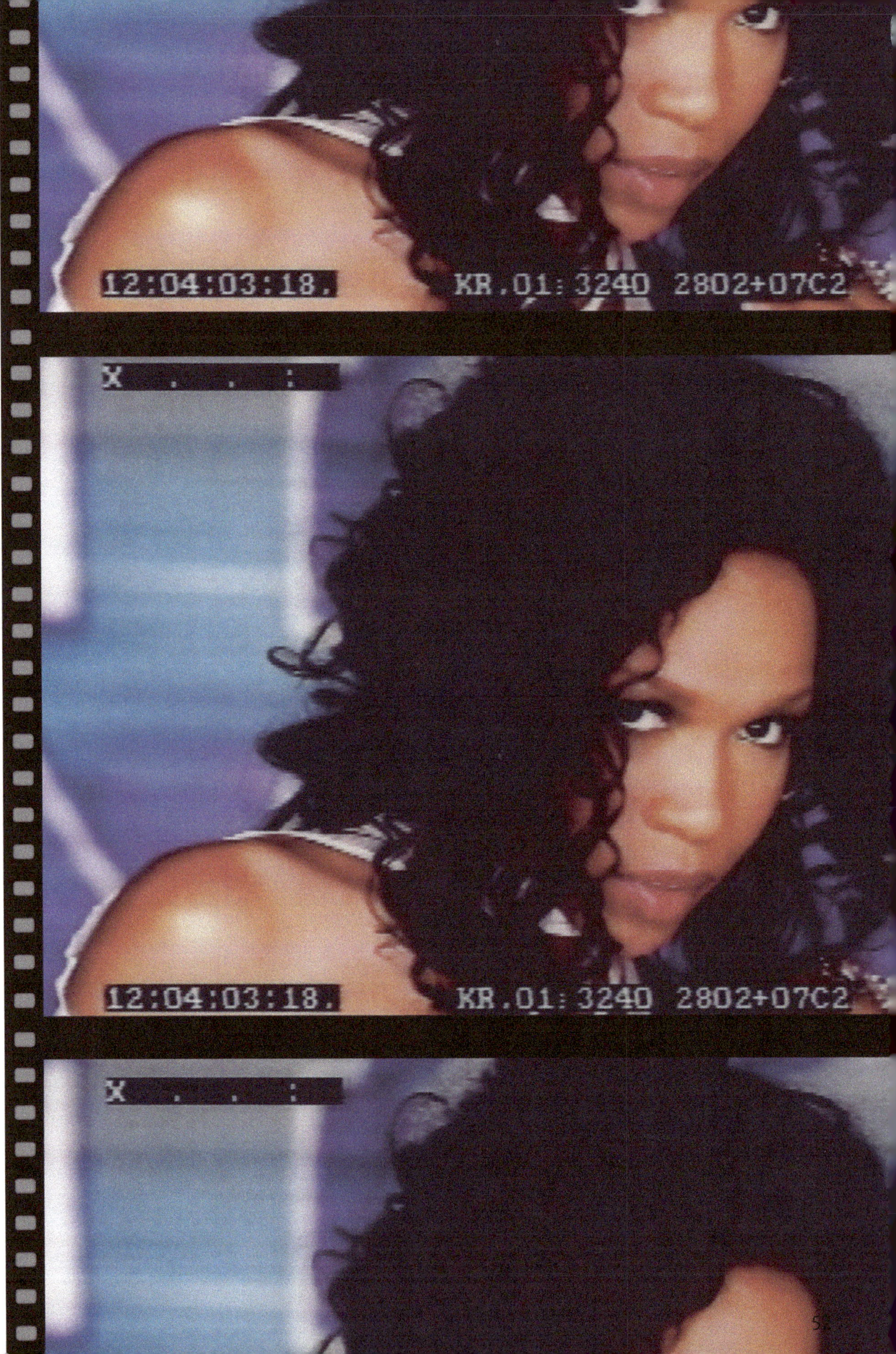

12:04:03:18.   KR.01: 3240 2802+07C2
12:04:03:18.   KR.01: 3240 2802+07C2

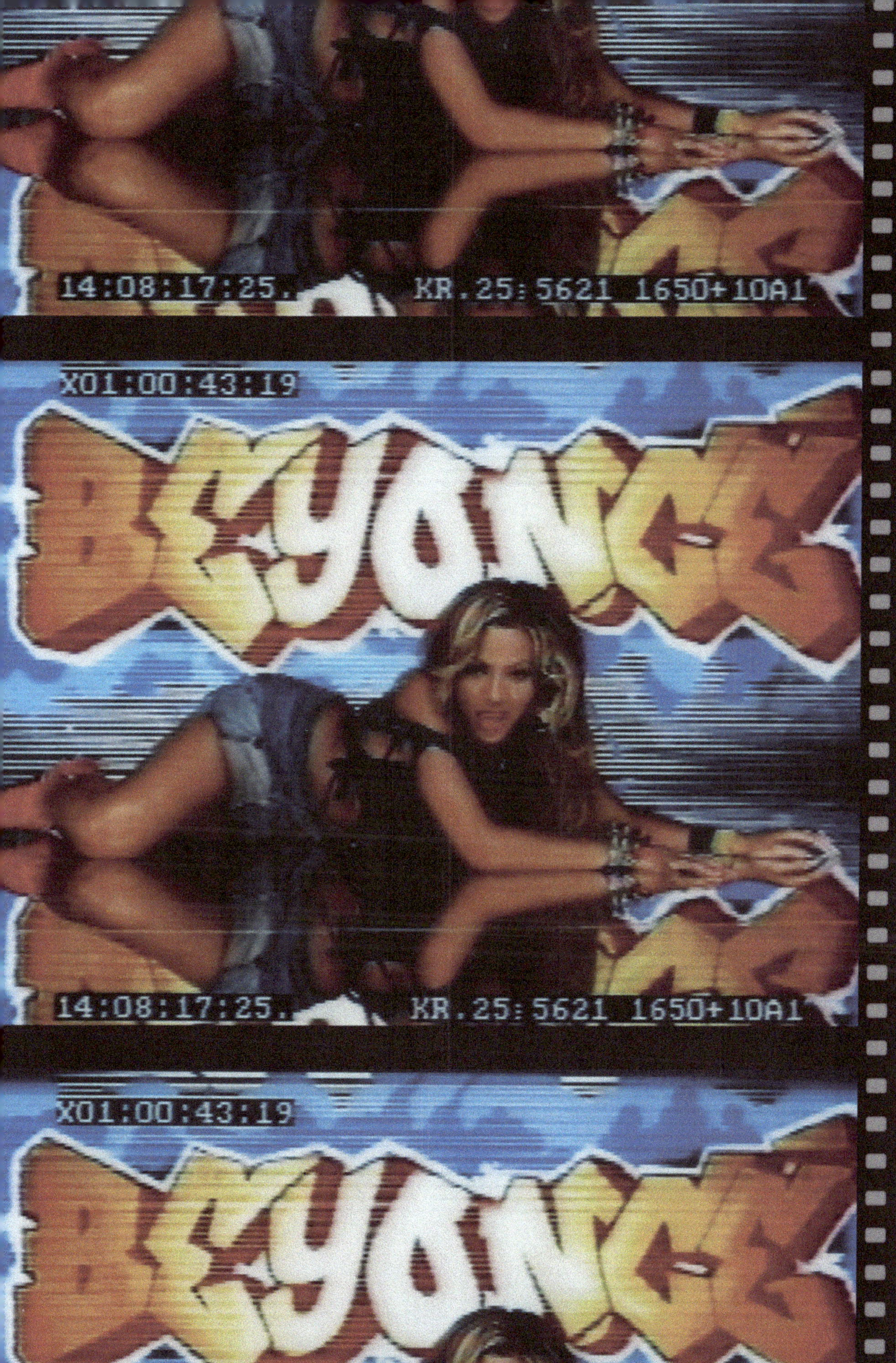
14:08:17:25.   KR.25:5621 1650+10A1
XO1:00:43:19
14:08:17:25.   KR.25:5621 1650+10A1
XO1:00:43:19

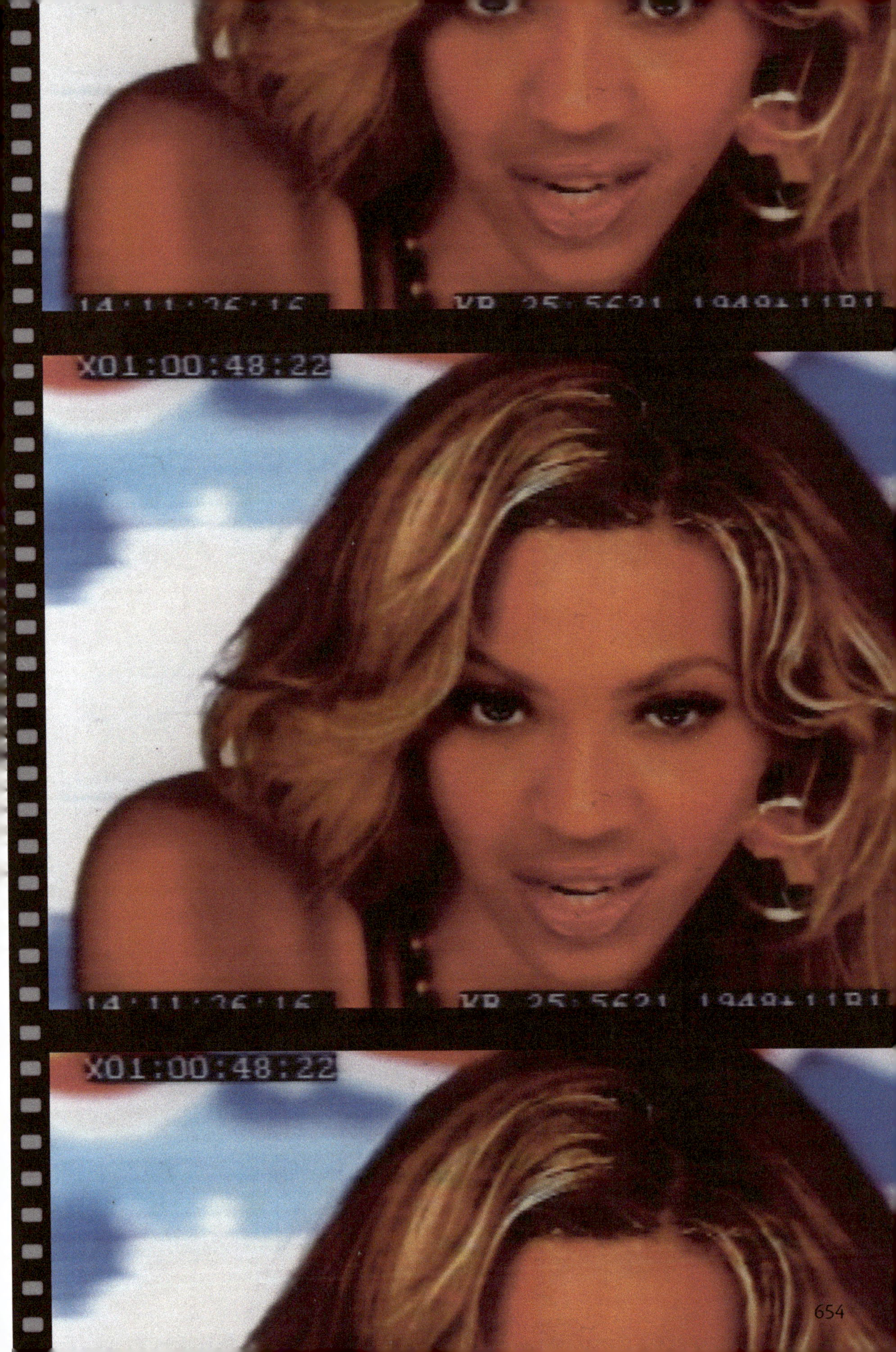

X01:00:48:22

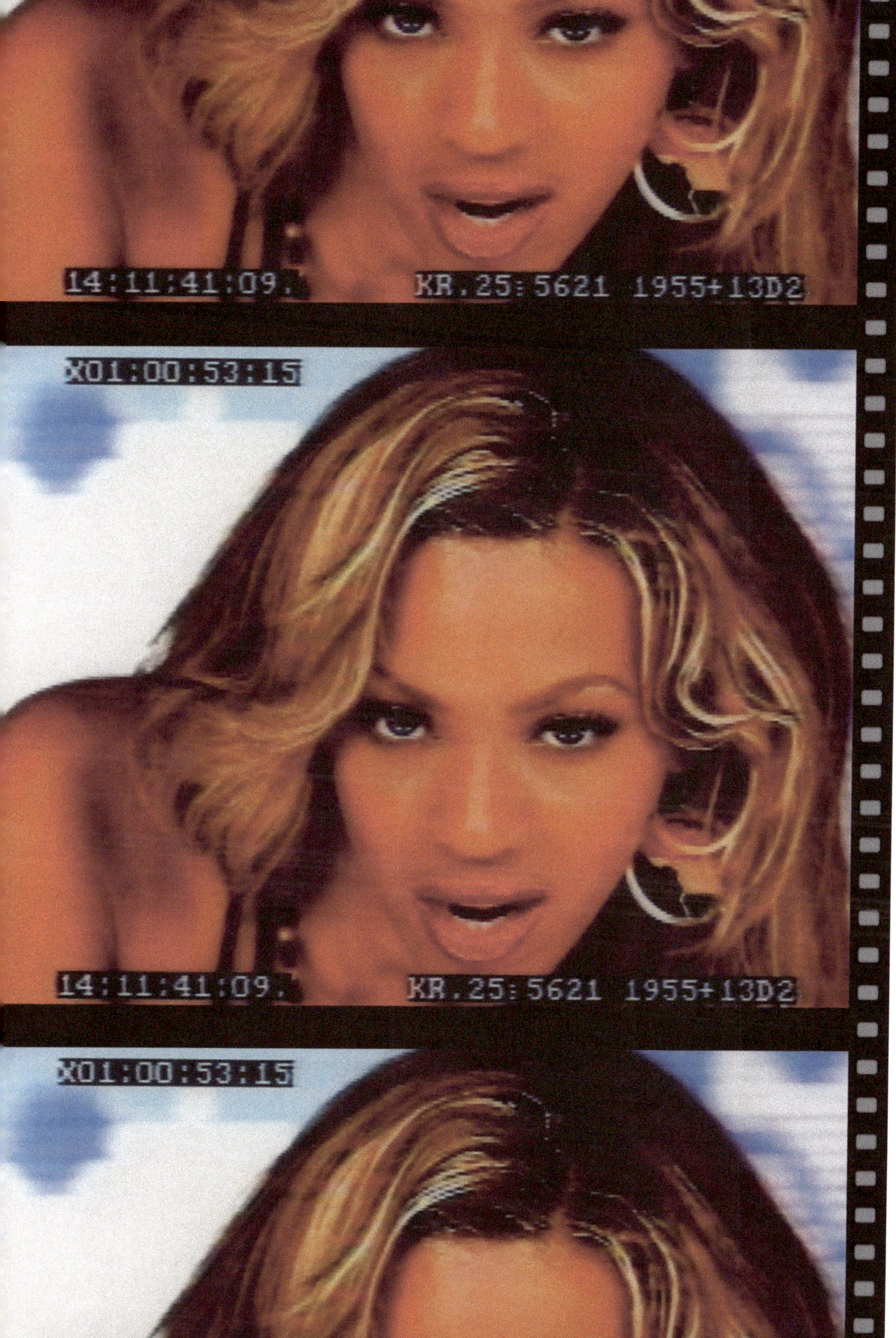

14:11:41:09.   KR.25:5621 1955+13D2
X01:00:53:15
14:11:41:09.   KR.25:5621 1955+13D2
X01:00:53:15

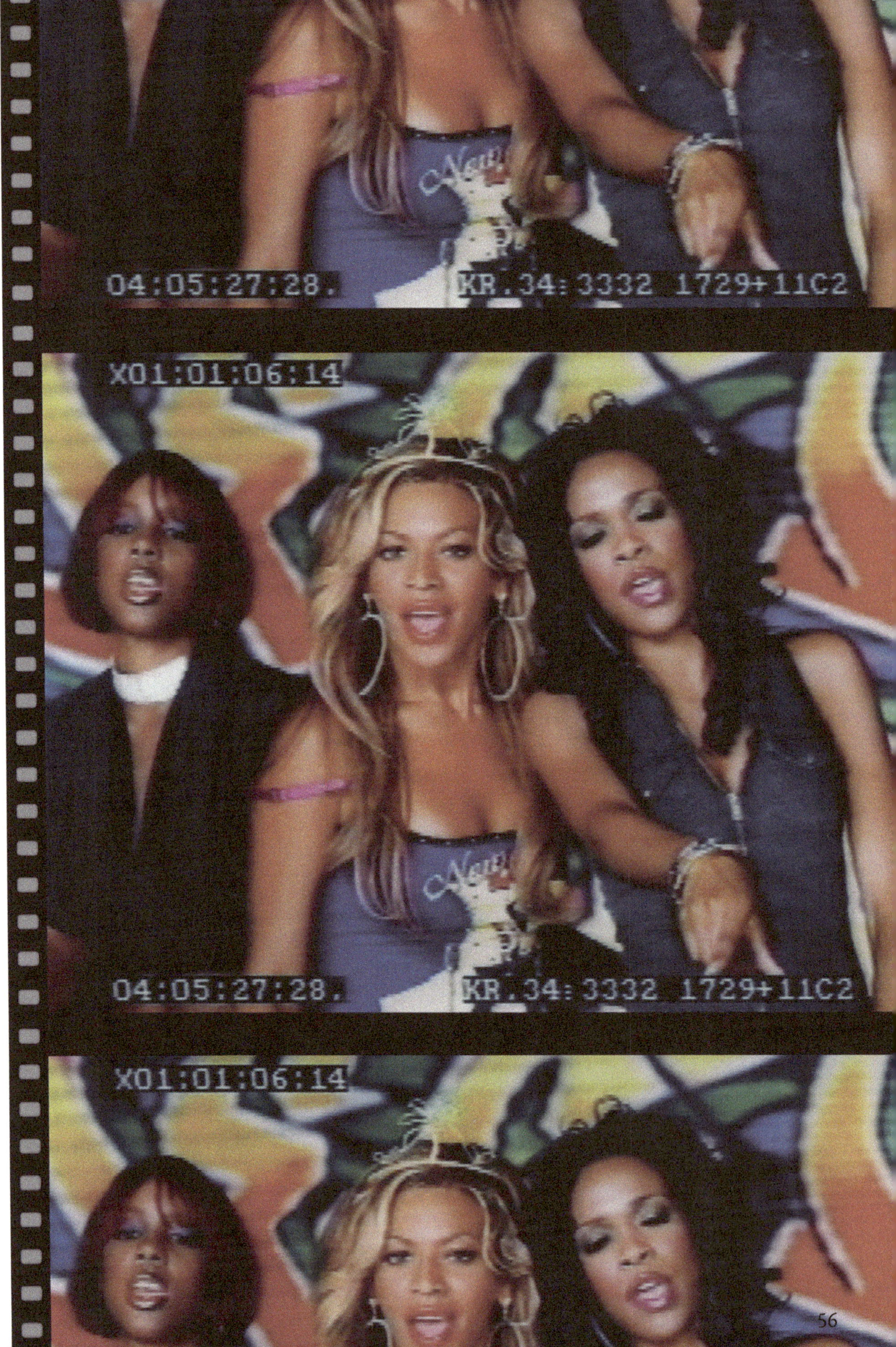
04:05:27:28.   KR.34: 3332 1729+11C2
X01:01:06:14
04:05:27:28.   KR.34: 3332 1729+11C2
X01:01:06:14

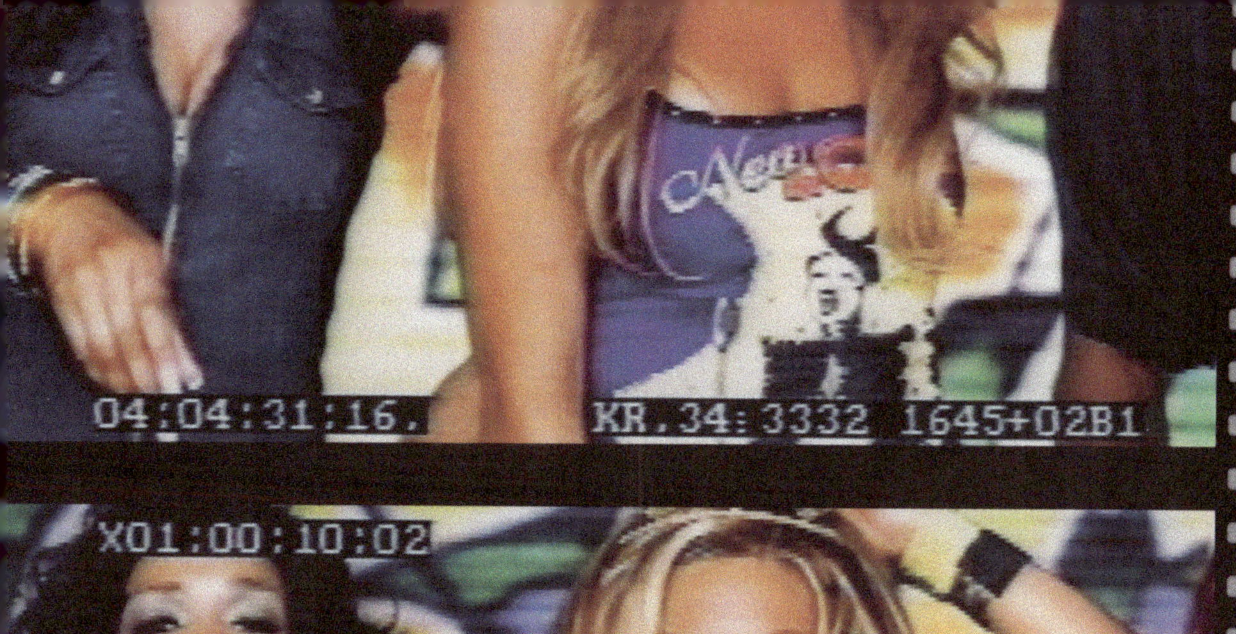

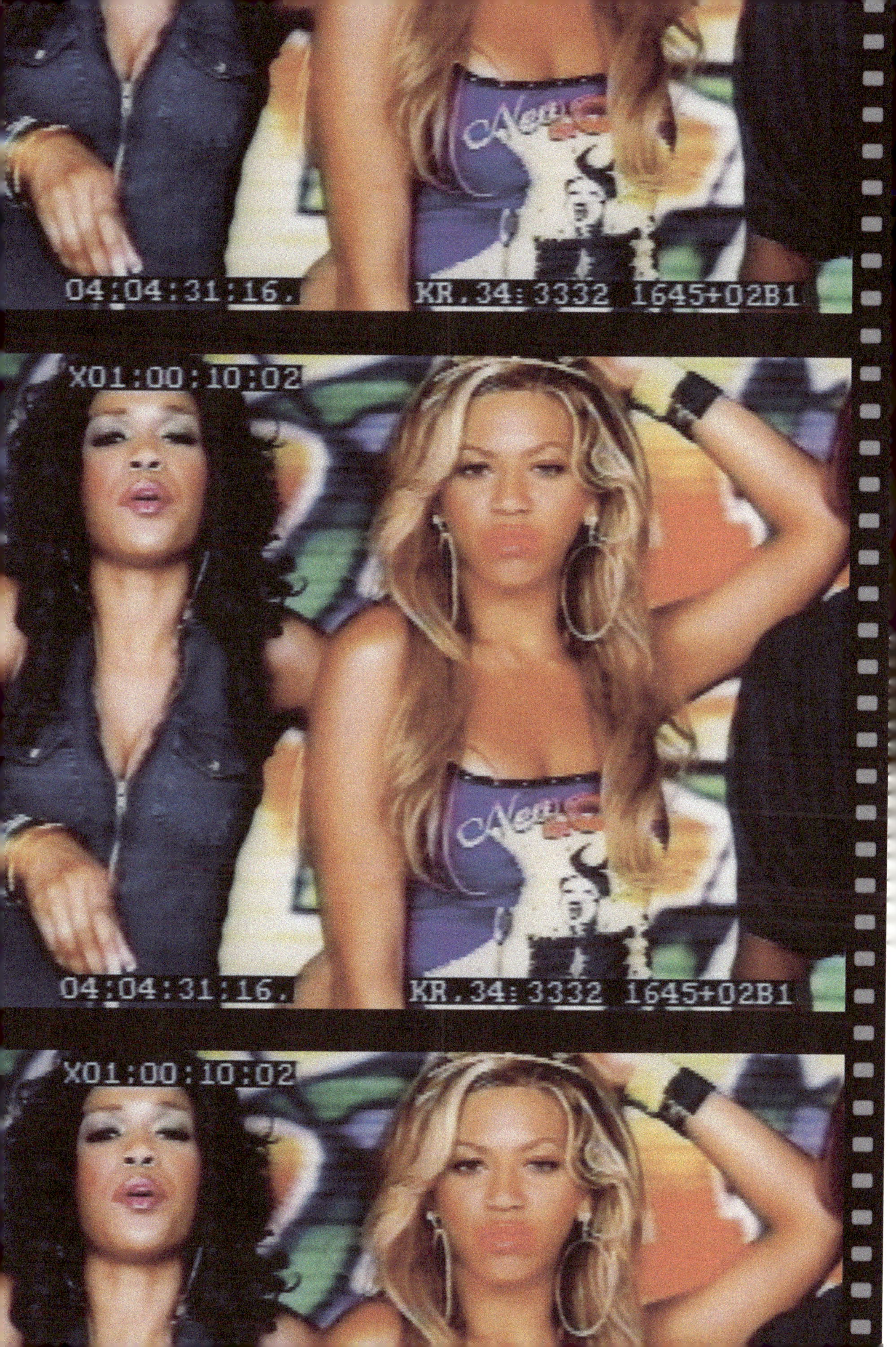

04:04:31:16.   KR.34: 3332 1645+02B1

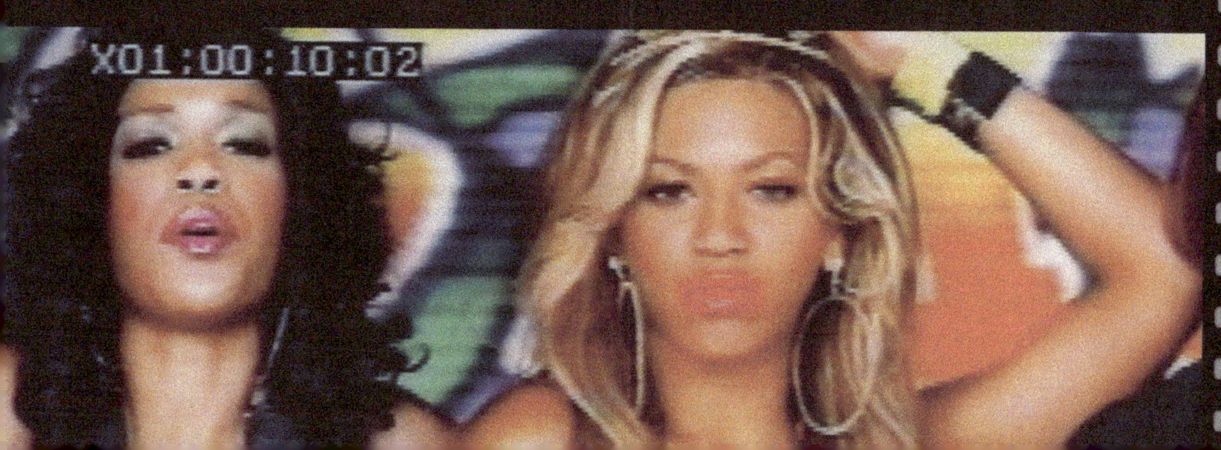

X01:00:10:02
04:04:31:16.   KR.34: 3332 1645+02B1
X01:00:10:02

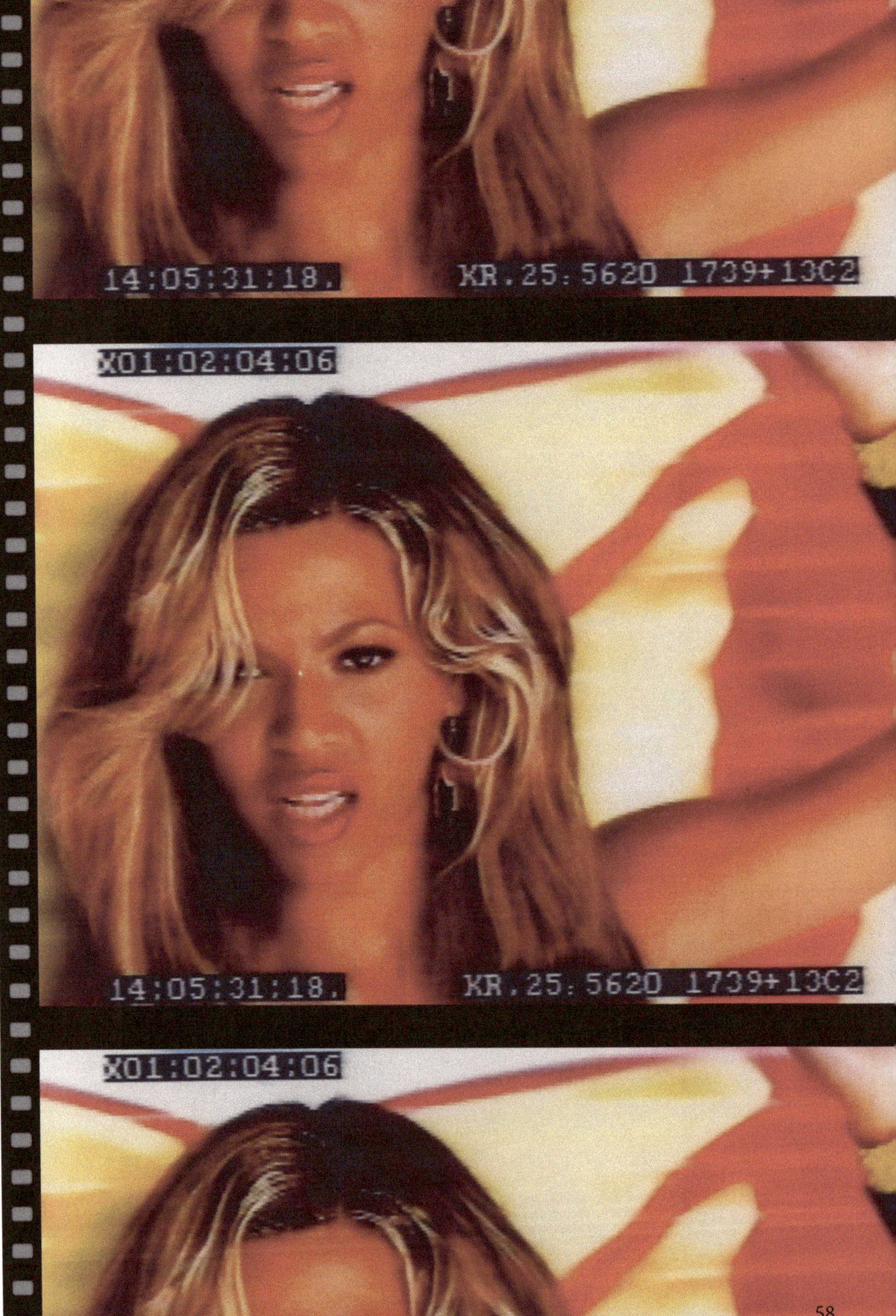

14:05:31:18.   KR.25: 5620 1739+13C2
X01:02:04:06
14:05:31:18.   KR.25: 5620 1739+13C2
X01:02:04:06

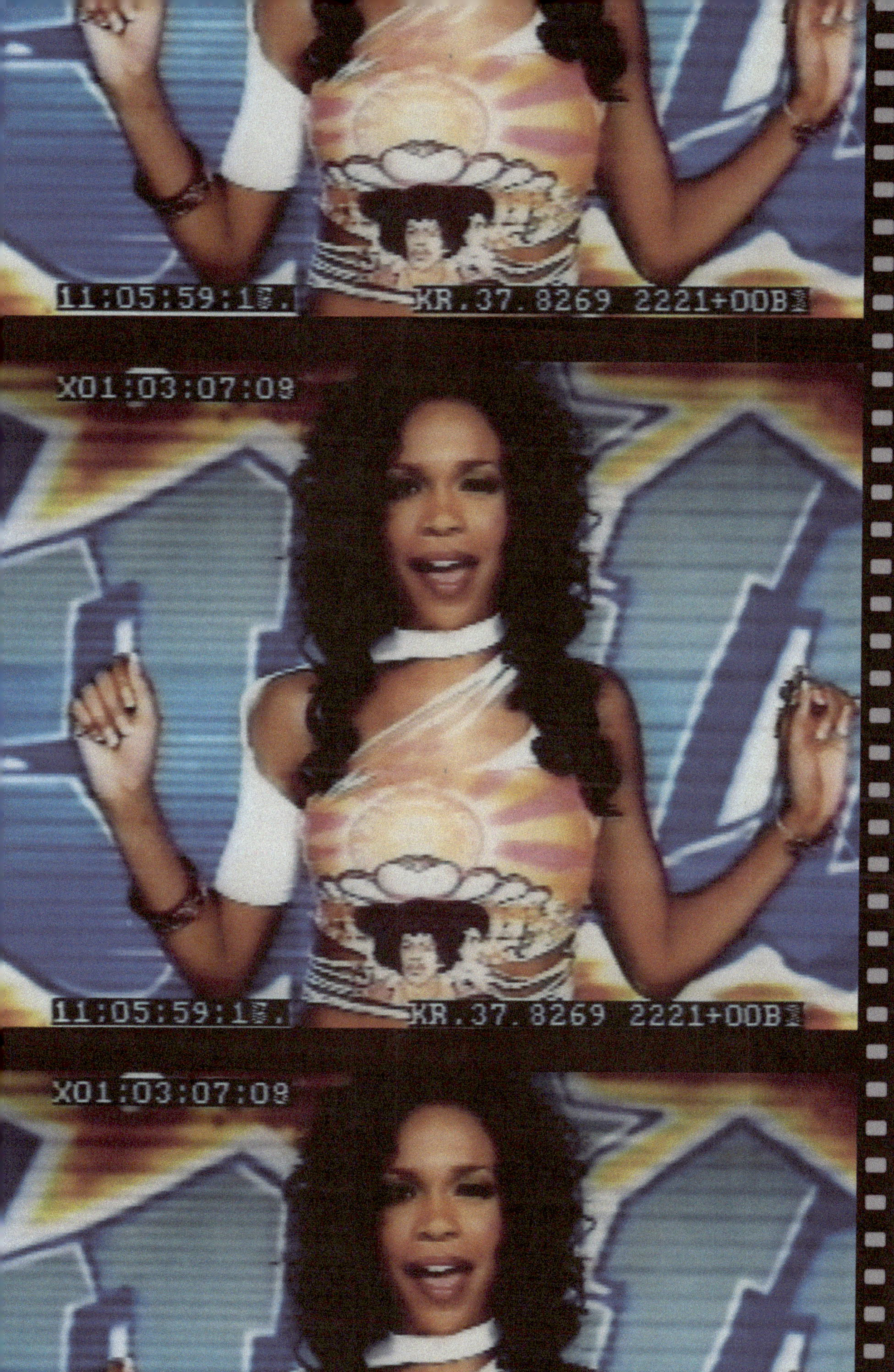

11:05:59:1 KR.37.8269 2221+00B
X01:03:07:09
11:05:59:1 KR.37.8269 2221+00B
X01:03:07:09

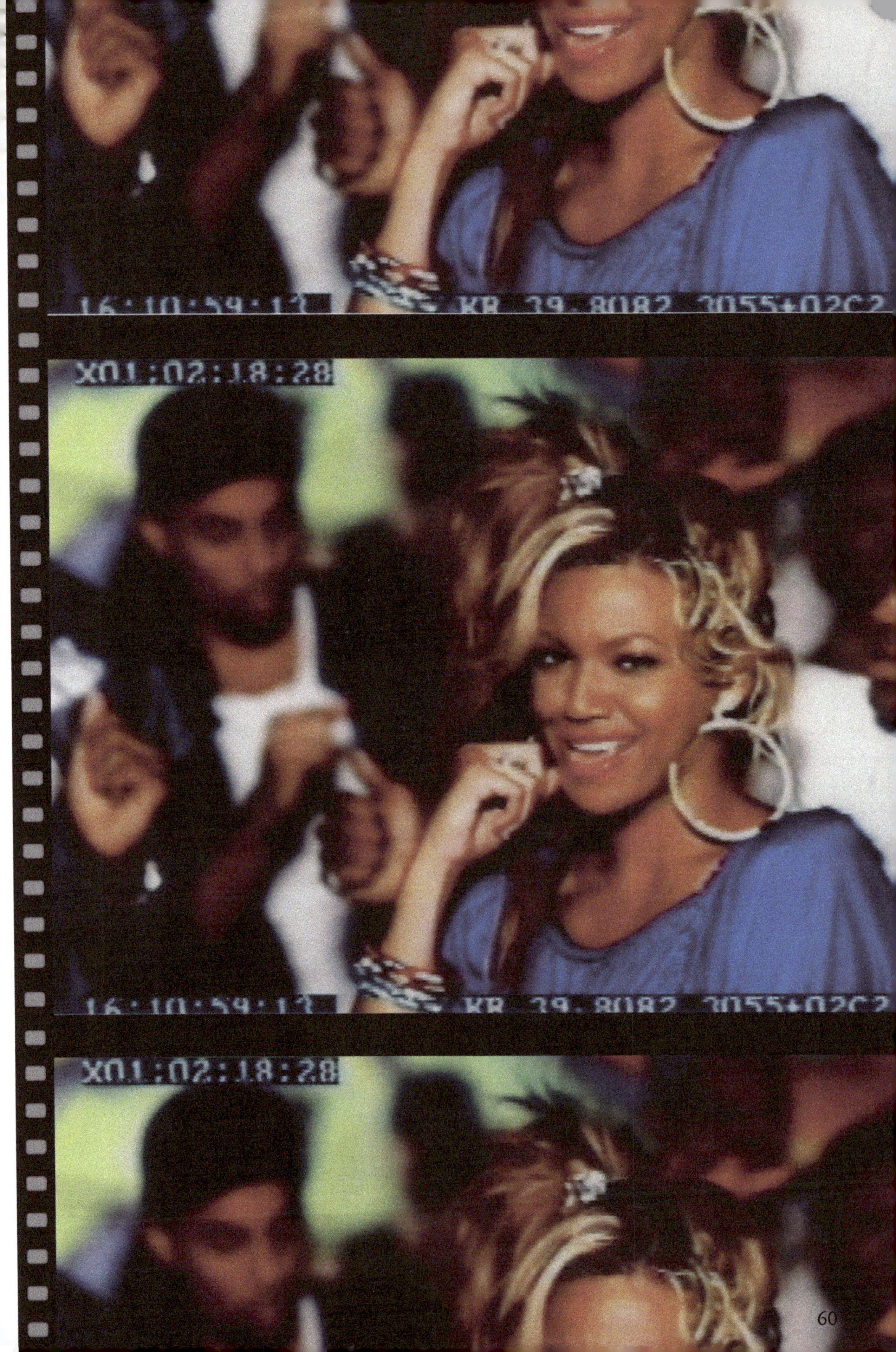

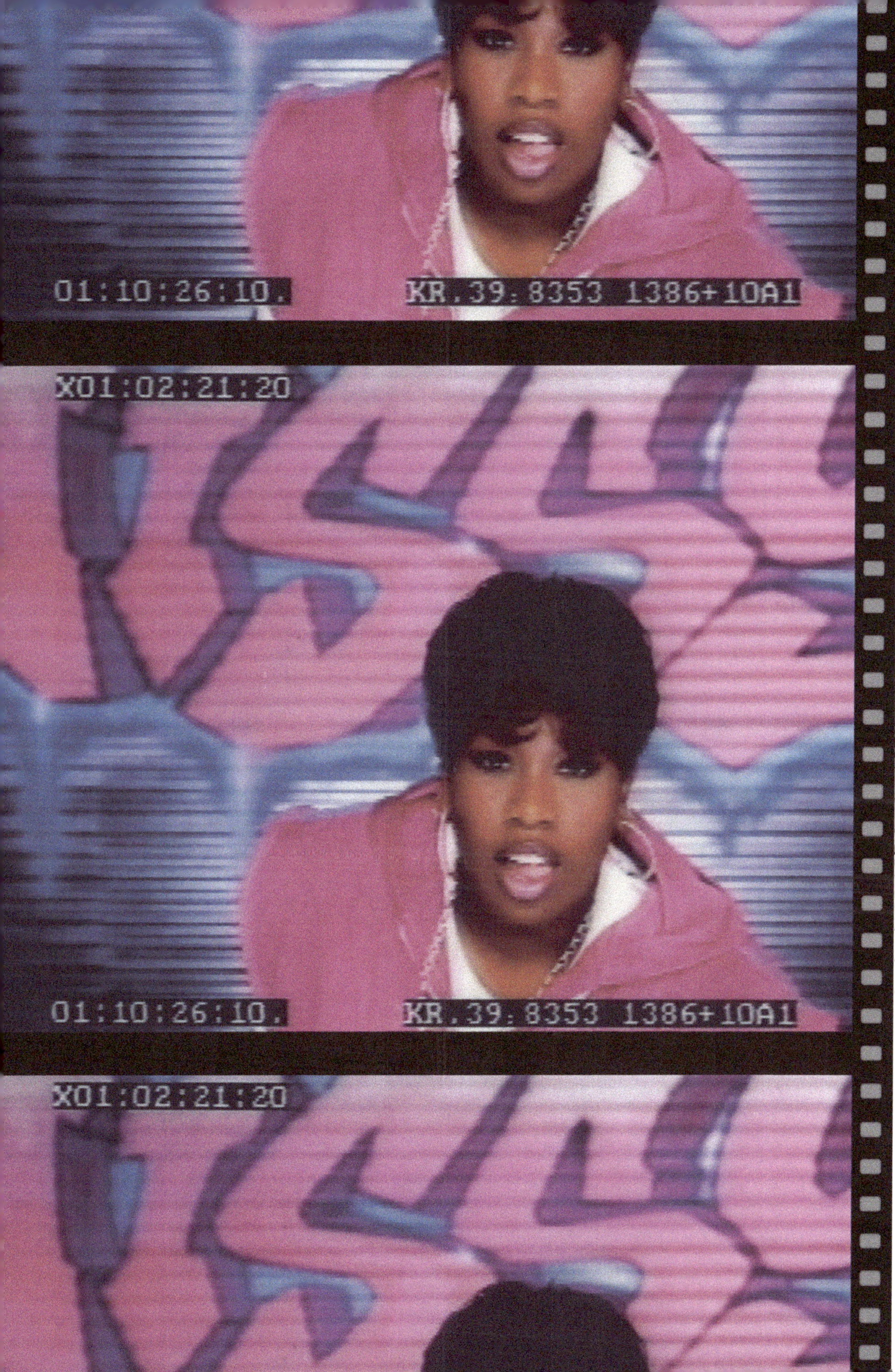
01:10:26:10.
KR.39:8353 1386+10A1
X01:02:21:20
01:10:26:10.
KR.39:8353 1386+10A1
X01:02:21:20

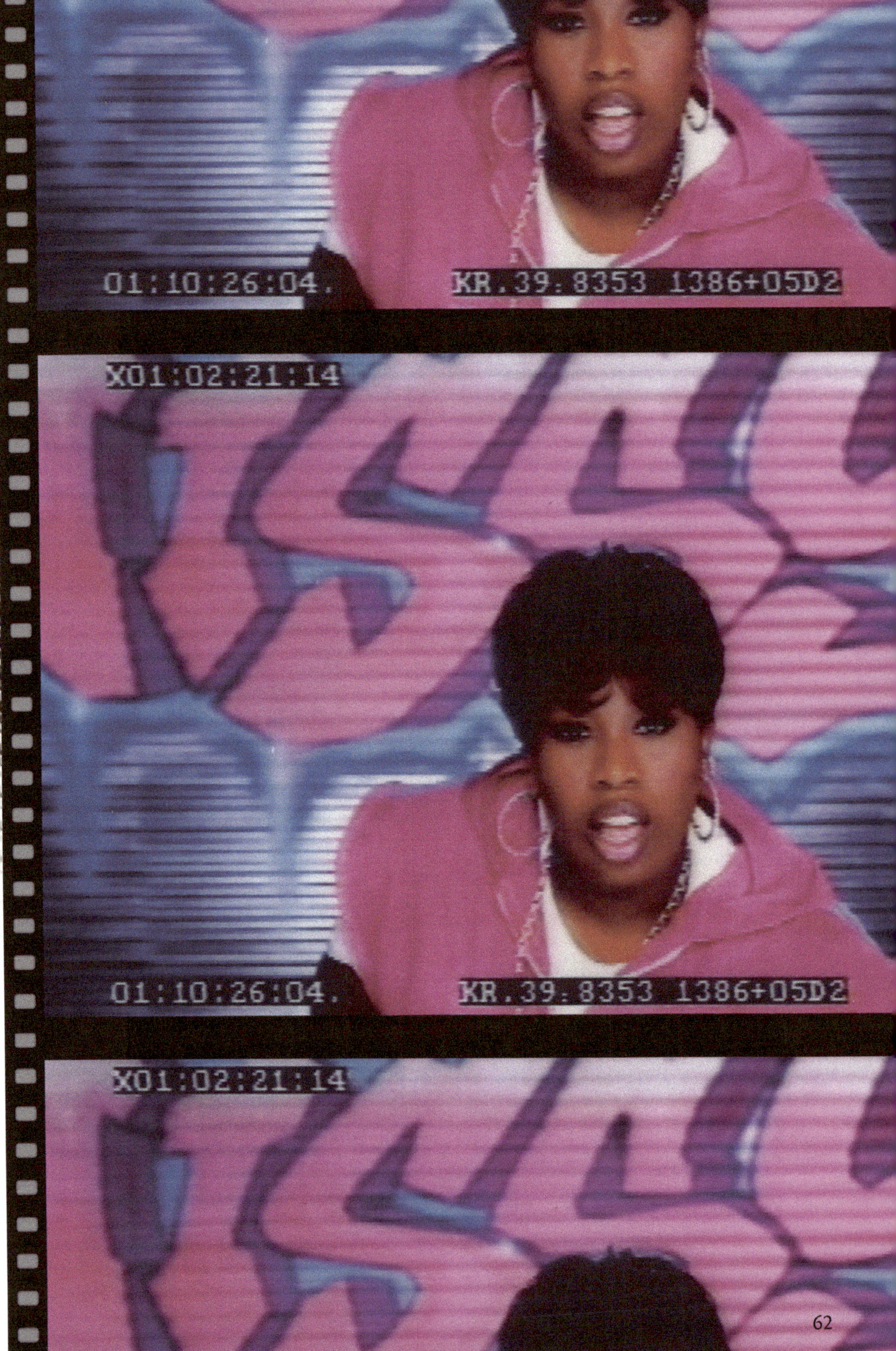

01:10:26:04.
KR.39. 8353 1386+05D2
X01:02:21:14
01:10:26:04.
KR.39. 8353 1386+05D2
X01:02:21:14

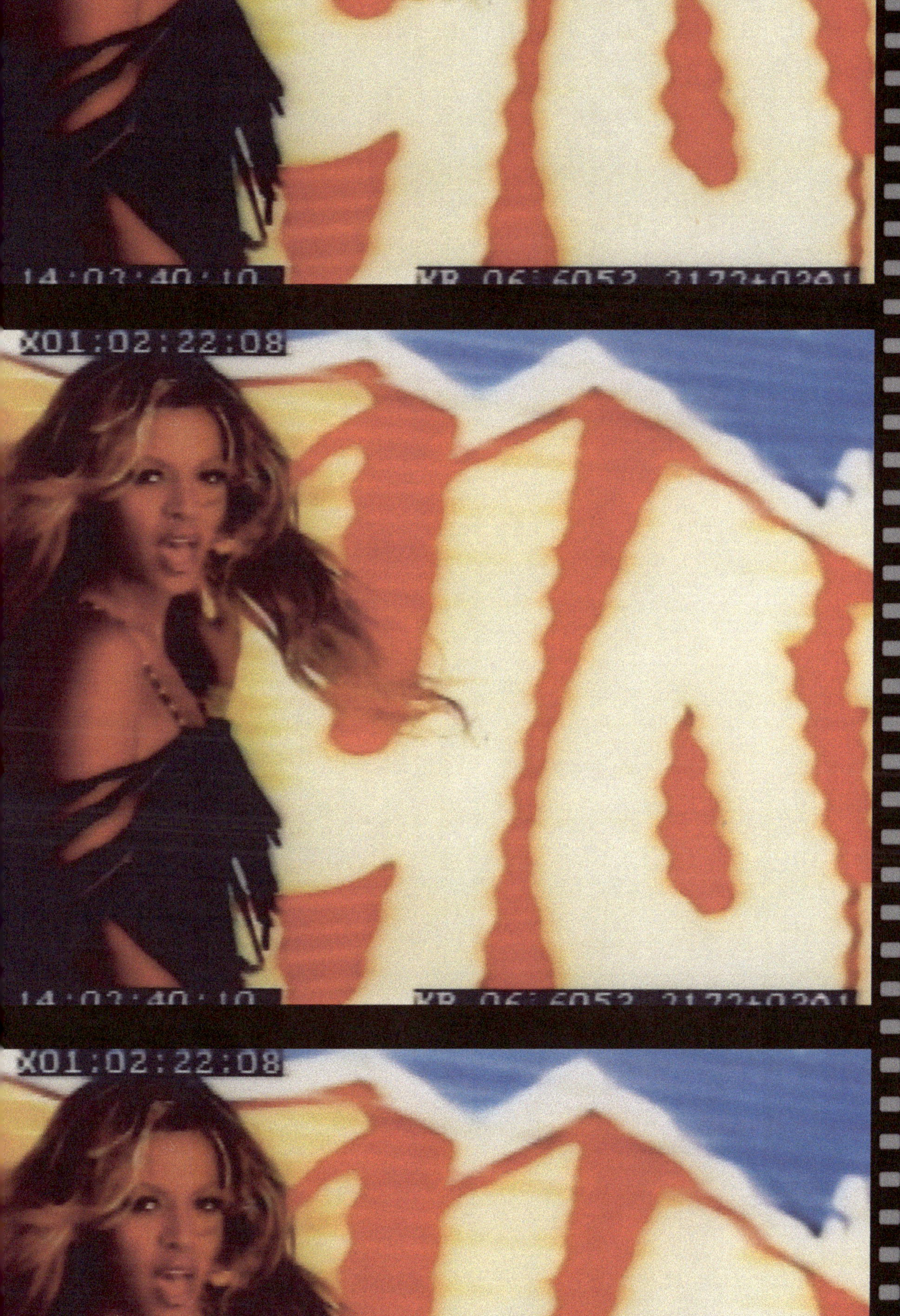

14:02:40:10
KR 06:6053 2172402601
X01:02:22:08
14:02:40:10
KR 06:6053 2172402601
X01:02:22:08

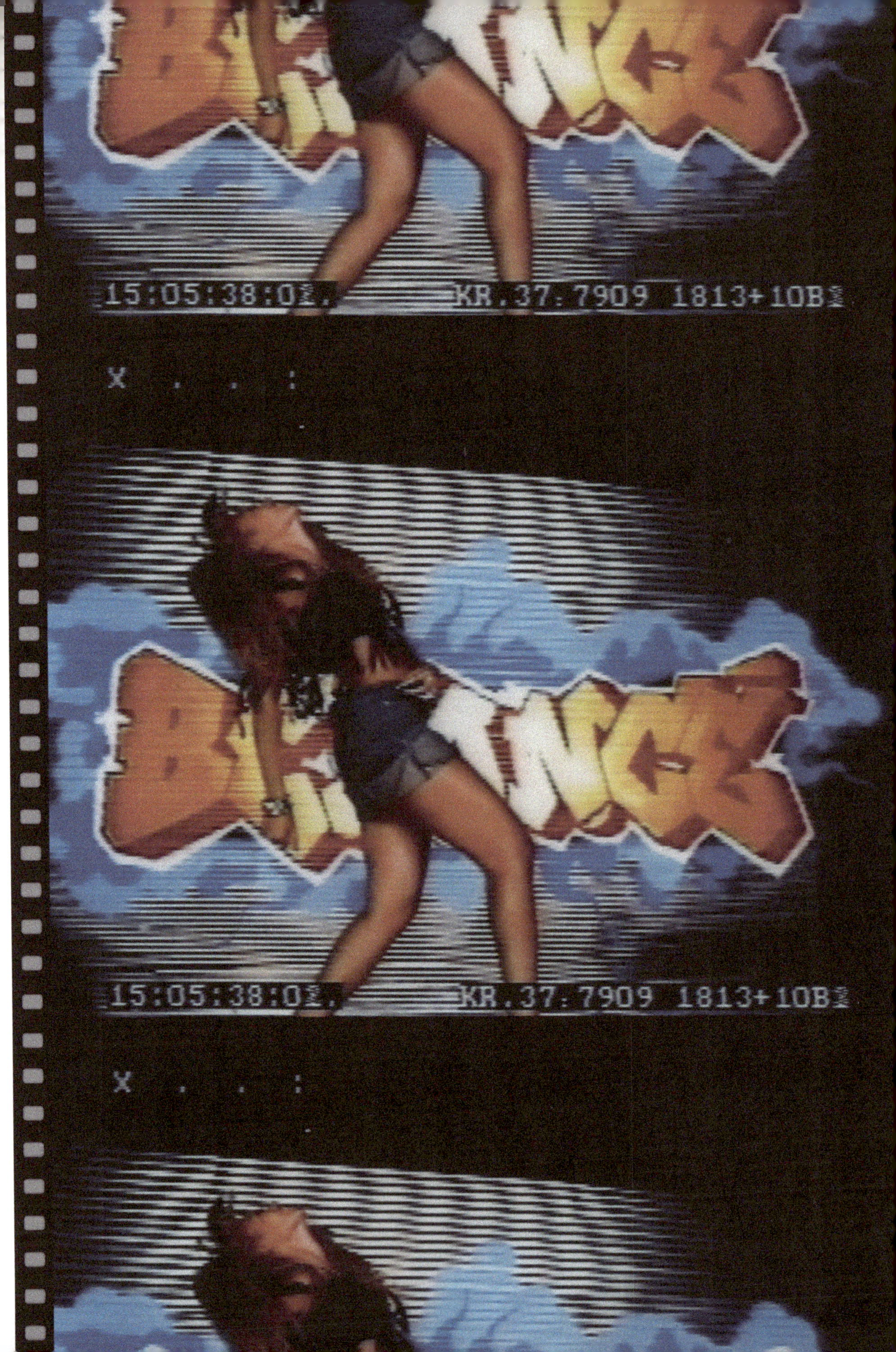

15:05:38:0   KR.37.7909 1813+10B
15:05:38:0   KR.37.7909 1813+10B

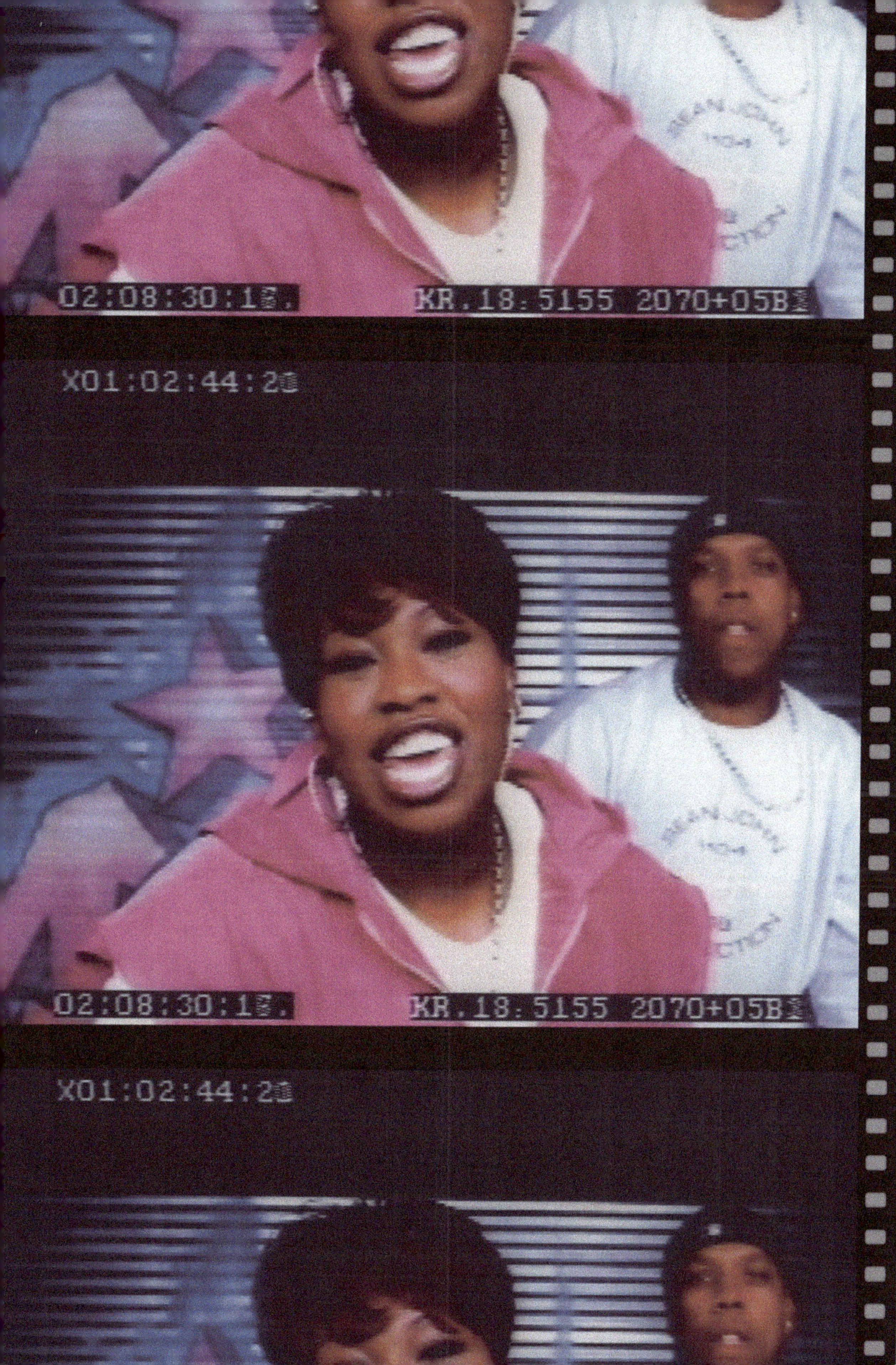

02:08:30:1
KR.18:5155 2070+05B
X01:02:44:20
02:08:30:1
KR.18:5155 2070+05B
X01:02:44:20

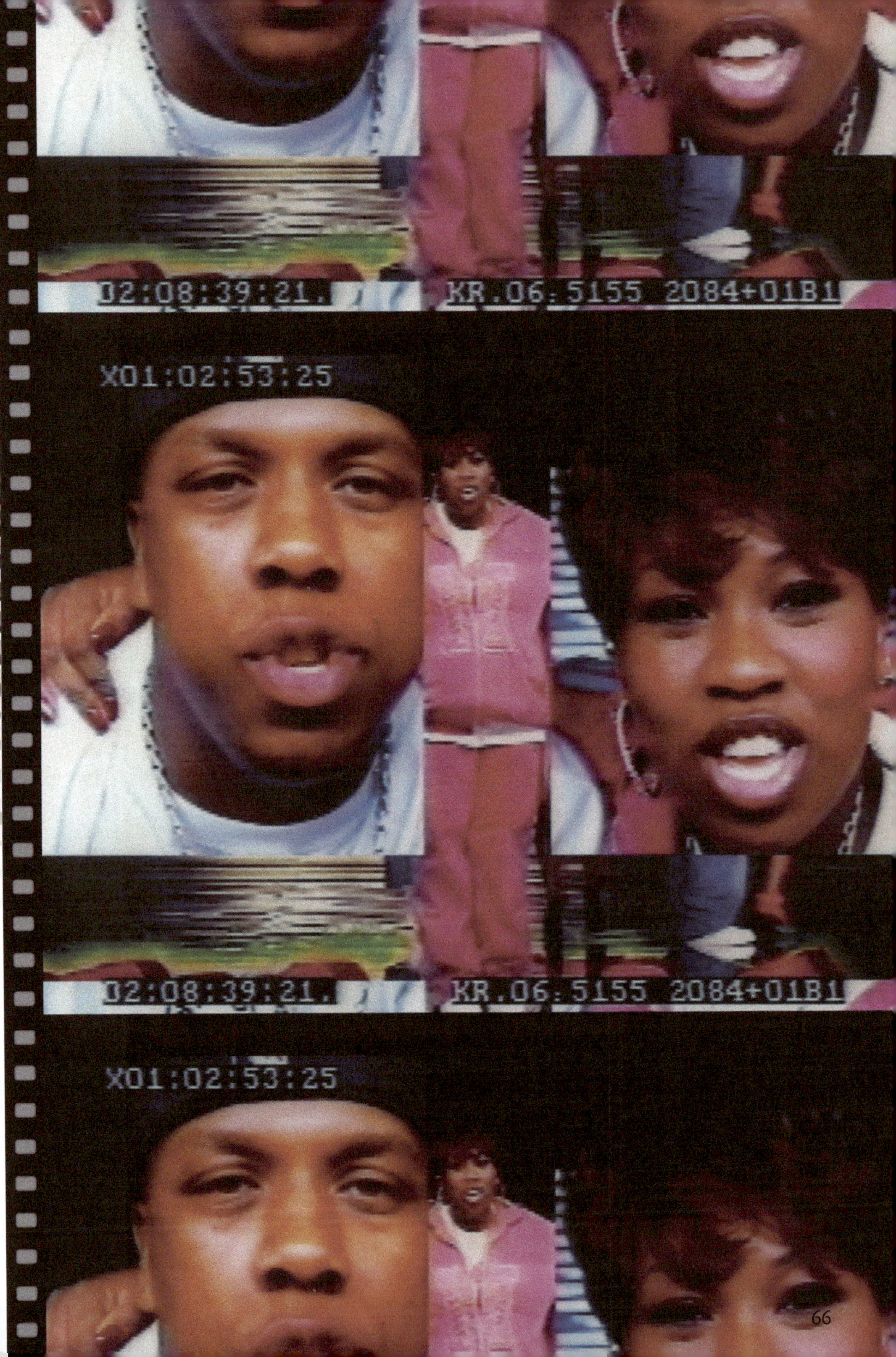

02:08:39:21.   KR.06:5155 2084+01B1
X01:02:53:25
02:08:39:21.   KR.06:5155 2084+01B1
X01:02:53:25

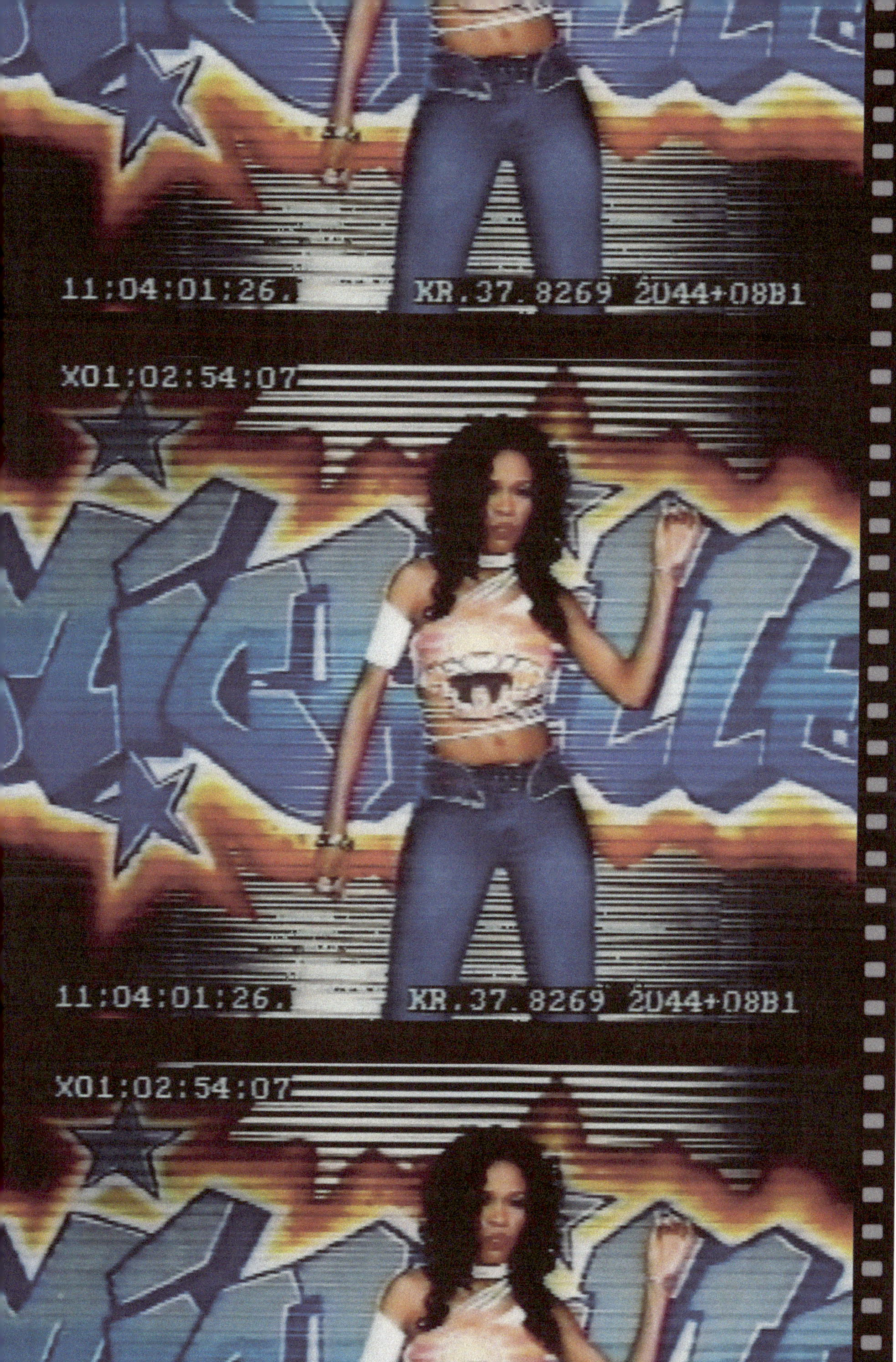

11:04:01:26.   KR.37.8269 2044+08B1
X01:02:54:07
11:04:01:26.   KR.37.8269 2044+08B1
X01:02:54:07

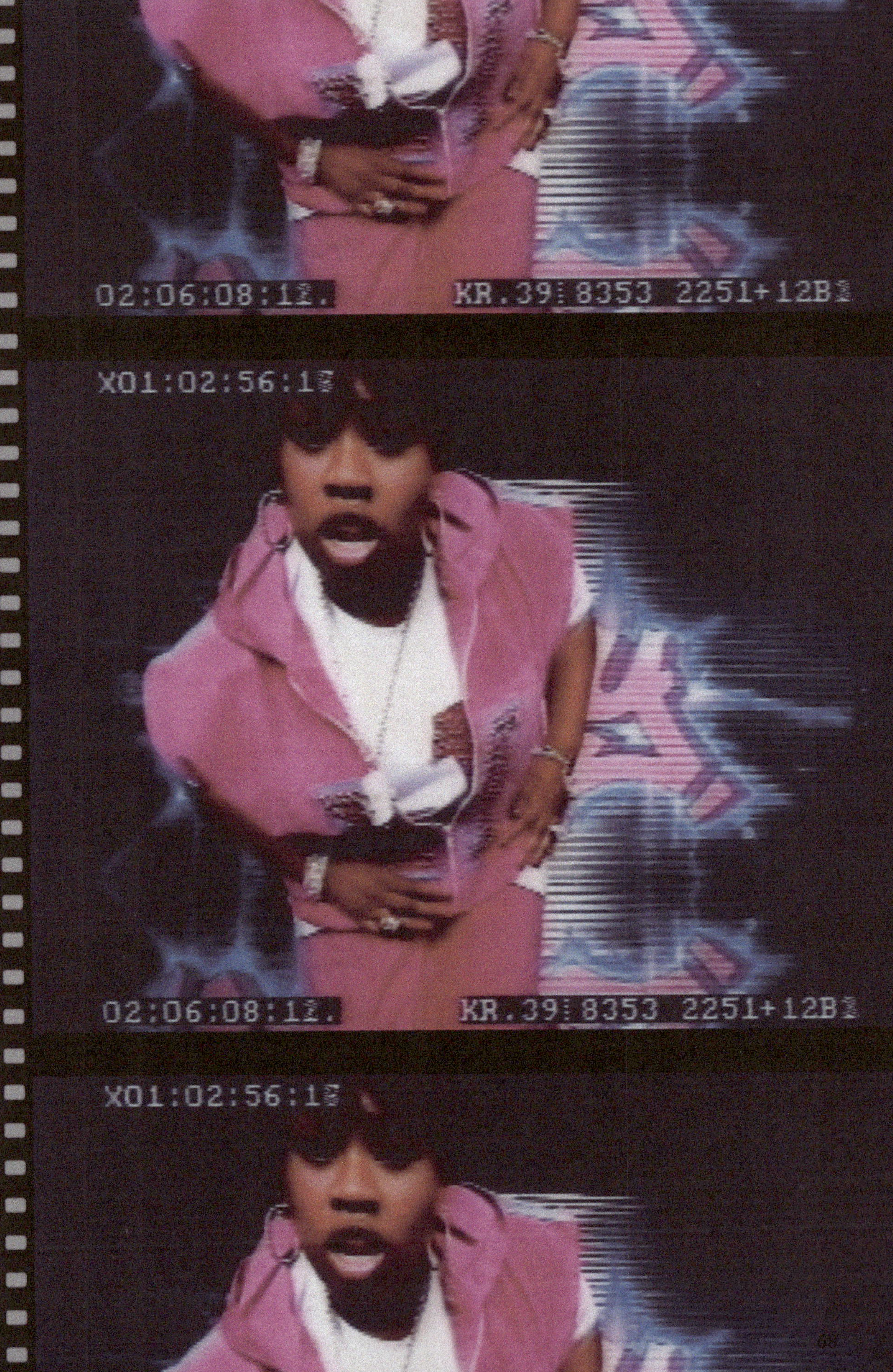
02:06:08:1⅔.   KR.39 8353 2251+12B
XO1:02:56:1⅔
02:06:08:1⅔.   KR.39 8353 2251+12B
XO1:02:56:1⅔

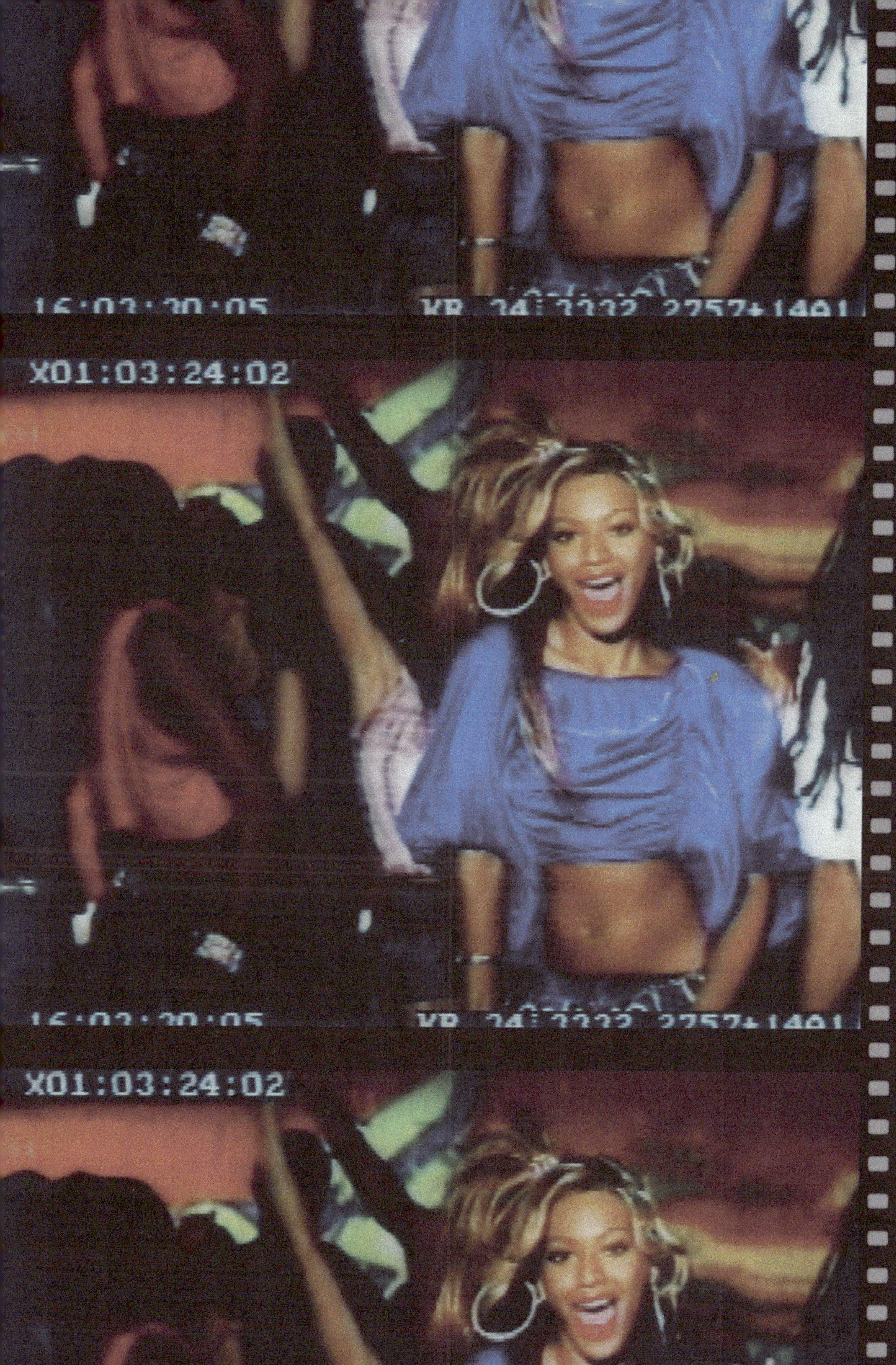

16:03:30:05
XO1:03:24:02
XO1:03:24:02

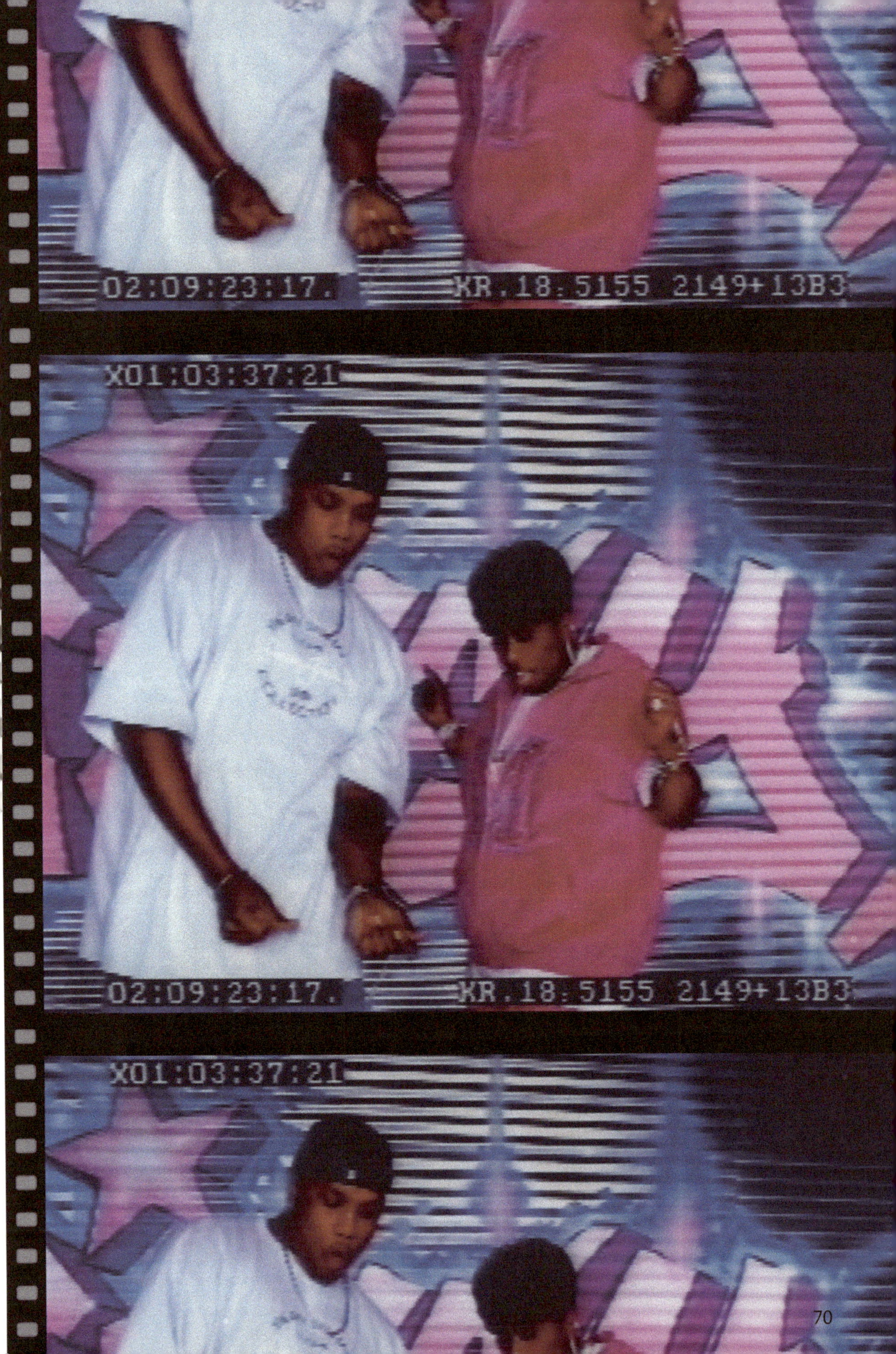

70

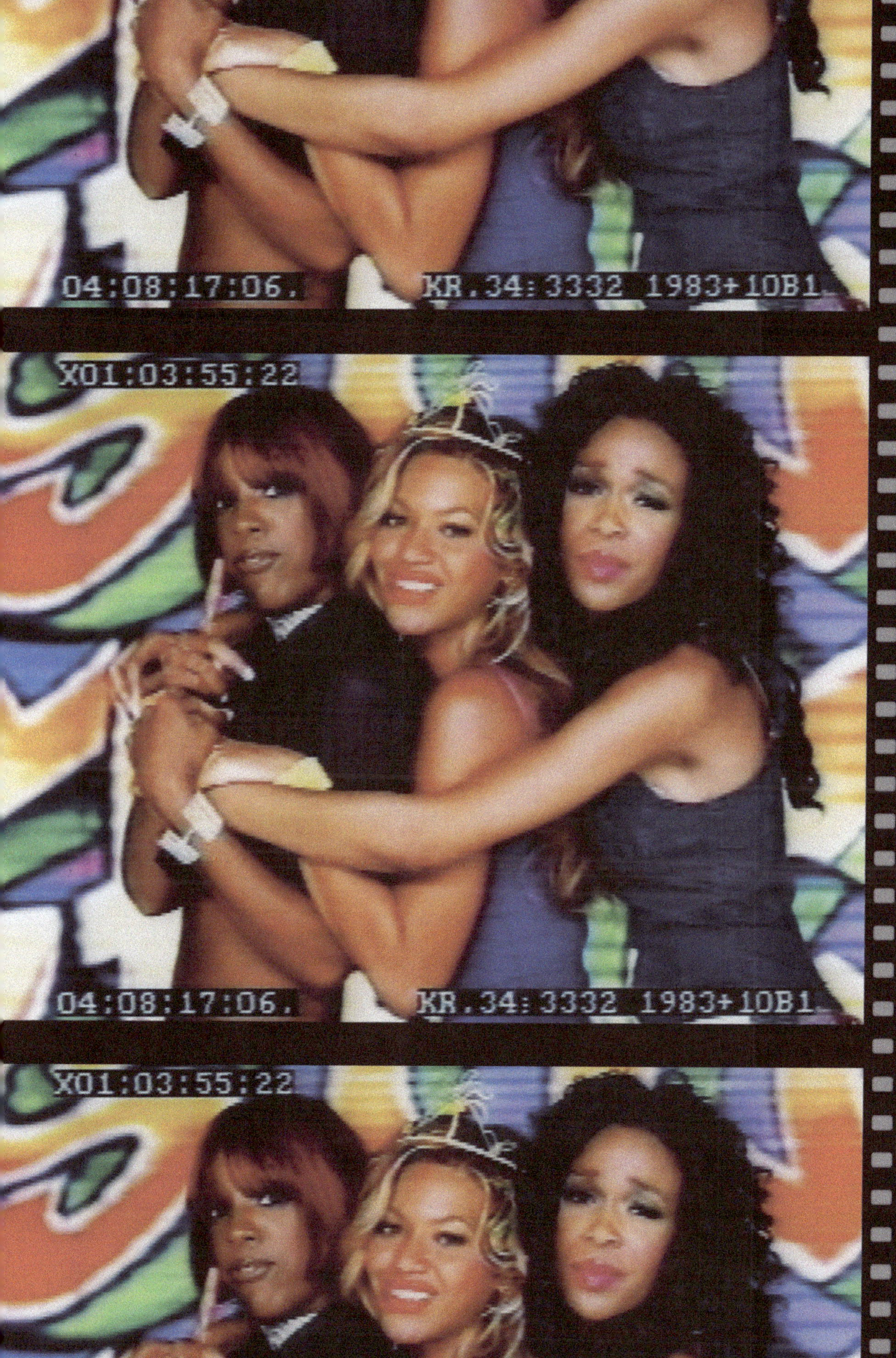

04:08:17:06.   KR.34:3332 1983+10B1
X01:03:55:22
04:08:17:06.   KR.34:3332 1983+10B1
X01:03:55:22

ALBUM DISCOGRAPHY

Destiny's Child

- ***Destiny's Child*** – *February 17, 1998 (Columbia Records)*

- ***The Writing's On The Wall*** – *July 27, 1999 (Columbia Records)*

- ***The Platinum's On The Wall*** – *February 20, 2001*

- ***Survivor*** – *May 1, 2001 (Columbia Records)*

- ***Love: Destiny EP*** – *May 1, 2001 (Target exclusive) (Columbia Records)*

- ***8 Days Of Christmas*** – *October 30, 2001 (Columbia Records)*

- ***This Is The Remix*** – *March 12, 2002 (Columbia Records)*

- ***Destiny's Child World Tour*** – *June 10, 2003 (DVD)*

- ***Destiny Fulfilled*** – *November 10, 2004 (Columbia Records)*

- ***#1's*** – *October 25, 2005 (Columbia Records)*

- ***Destiny's Child: Live In Atlanta*** – *March 28, 2006 (Columbia Records)*

- ***Matthew Knowles & Music World Present Vol. 1: Love Destiny*** – *June 25, 2008 (Japan exclusive) (Columbia Records)*

- ***Playlist: The Very Best Of Destiny's Child*** – *October 9, 2012 (Columbia Records)*

- ***Love Songs*** – *January 29, 2013 (Columbia Records)*

- ***Destiny's Child Video Anthology*** – *May 31, 2013 (DVD) (Music World Entertainment/Columbia Records/Legacy)*

Beyoncé:

- ***Dangerously In Love*** – *June 23, 2003 (Columbia Records)*

- ***Live At Wembley*** – *April 26, 2004 (CD/DVD) (Columbia Records)*

- ***True Star: A Private Performance*** - *2004 (Limited Edition 5" CD single for Tommy Hilfiger fragrance campaign) (Sony Music)*

- ***B'Day*** – *August 31, 2006 (Sony Urban Music/Columbia Records)*

- ***The Beyoncé Experience Live*** – *November 16, 2007 (CD/DVD) (Columbia Records)*

- ***Irreemplazable*** – *August 28, 2008 (Columbia Records)*

- ***I Am... Sasha Fierce*** – *November 14, 2008 (Music World Entertainment/Columbia Records)*

- ***Dangerously In Love/Live at Wembley*** – *December 9, 2008 (CD/DVD) (Columbia Records)*

- ***Above and Beyoncé: Video Collection & Dance Mixes*** – *June 16, 2009 (CD/DVD) (Columbia Records)*

- ***I Am... Yours: An Intimate Performance at Wynn Las Vegas*** – *November 23, 2009 (CD/DVD) (Columbia Records)*

- ***I Am... World Tour*** – *November 26, 2010 (CD/DVD)*

- ***4*** – *June 24, 2011 (Parkwood Entertainment/Columbia Records)*

- ***4: The Remix*** – *April 23, 2012 (Digital) (Parkwood Entertainment/Columbia Records)*

- ***Beyoncé*** – *December 13, 2013 (Parkwood Entertainment/Columbia Records)*

- ***More Only*** – *November 24, 2014 (Digital) (Columbia Records)*

- ***Beyoncé: Platinum Edition*** – *November 24, 2014 (CD/DVD) (Parkwood Entertainment/Columbia Records)*

- ***Lemonade*** – *April 23, 2016 (Parkwood Entertainment/Columbia Records)*

Kelly Rowland

- *Simply Deep* – October 22, 2002 (Columbia Records)

- *Ms. Kelly* – June 22, 2007 (Columbia Records)

- *Ms. Kelly: Diva Deluxe EP* – May 25, 2008 (Columbia Records)

- *Ms. Kelly Deluxe Digital EP* – June 27, 2008 (Columbia Records)

- *Simply Deep/Ms. Kelly: Deluxe Edition* – September 27, 2010 (Columbia Records)

- *Word: The Very Best of Kelly Rowland* – October 25, 2010 (Camden/Sony Music)

- *Here I Am* – July 26, 2011 (Universal/Motown)

- *Playlist: The Very Best of Kelly Rowland* – October 18, 2011 (Sony Legacy)

- *Talk A Good Game* – June 14, 2013 (Republic)

LeToya Luckett

- *LeToya* – July 25, 2006 (Capitol Records)

- *Lady Love* – August 25, 2009 (Capitol Records)

- *Until Ten* – (TBD) September 2016 (eOne)

SINGLES

- "No, No, No" featuring Wyclef Jean - November 11, 1997

- "With Me" featuring Jermaine Dupri – January 20, 1998

- "Get On The Bus" featuring Timbaland – September 29, 1998

- "Bills, Bills, Bills" - June 14, 1999

- "Bug A Boo" - August 23, 1999

- "Say My Name" - November 7, 1999

- "Jumpin' Jumpin'" - July 4, 2000

- "Independent Women Part I" - September 4, 2000

- "Survivor" - February 13, 2001

- "Bootylicious" - May 20, 2001

- "Emotion" - October 8, 2001

- "8 Days of Christmas" - December 16, 2001

- "Nasty Girl" - March 25, 2002

- "Lose My Breath" - September 21, 2004

- "Soldier" featuring T.I. and Lil' Wayne – December 7, 2004

- "Girl" - April 25, 2005

- "Cater 2 U" - June 14, 2005

- "Stand Up For Love" - September 27, 2005

FEATURED ARTIST

- **Lil' O** featuring Destiny's Child – "Can't Stop" 1997

- **Silkk the Shocker** featuring Destiny's Child and Master P - "Just Be Straight With Me" - January 23, 1998

- **Matthew Marsden** featuring Destiny's Child – "She's Gone" 1998

- **Jessica Simpson** featuring Destiny's Child - "Woman In Me" - Sweet Kisses - November 23, 1999

- **50 Cent featuring** Destiny's Child - "Thug Love" - September 21, 1999

- **Mary Mary** featuring Destiny's Child - "Good To Me" - Thankful - May 2, 2000

- **Cam'Ron** featuring Jim Jones and Destiny's Child - "Do It Again" - S.D.E. September 19, 2000

- **99 Souls** featuring Destiny's Child and Brandy - "The Girl Is Mine" - November 6, 2015

SOUNDTRACKS

- **Men In Black** - "Killing Time" - July 1, 1997 (Columbia Records/Sony)

- **Why Do Fools Fall In Love** - "Get On The Bus" featuring Timbaland – September 8, 1998 (Elektra Records/East/West Records/The Gold Mind, Inc.)

- **NFL Jams '98** - "Once A Fool" featuring William Floyd – September 29, 1998 (Intersound Records)

- **Life** - "Stimulate Me" featuring Mocha – March 16, 1999 (Rock Land/Interscope)

- **The PJs** - "No More Rainy Days" - March 30, 1999 (Hollywood Records)

- **Big Momma's House** - "Big Momma's Theme" Da Brat featuring Vita – May 30, 2000 (So So Def)

- **Romeo Must Die** - "Perfect Man" - March 28, 2000 (Blackground Records)

- **Charlie's Angels** - "Independent Women" and "Dot" - October 24, 2000 (Sony)

- **MTV's Hip Hopera: Carmen** - "Survivor" Extended Remix featuring Da Brat and "Bootylicious" Rockwilder Remix featuring Missy Elliott – June 12, 2001 (Sony)

- **The Fighting Temptations** - "I Know" - September 9, 2003 (Music World Entertainment/Columbia Records/Sony)

MUSIC VIDEOS

1997

- "Can't Stop" Lil' O featuring Destiny's Child
  "No, No, No" (Part II) featuring Wyclef Jean

1998

- "No, No, No" (Part I)
  "With Me" featuring Jermaine Dupri
  "Get On The Bus" featuring Timbaland
  "Just Be Straight With Me" Silkk The Shocker featuring Destiny's Child and Master P
  She's Gone" Matthew Marsden featuring Destiny's Child

1999

"Bills, Bills, Bills"
"Bug A Boo"

2000

- "Say My Name"
- "Jumpin' Jumpin'"
- "Jumpin' Jumpin'" [So So Def Remix] featuring Jermaine Dupri, Da Brat and Lil Bow Wow
- "Independent Women [Part I]

2001

- "Survivor" [Remix] featuring Da Brat
- "Emotion"
- "8 Days of Christmas"
- Bootylicious
- Bootylicious (Remix) featuring Missy Elliot & Rockwilder

2002

- "Nasty Girl"

2004

•"Lose My Breath"
"Soldier" featuring T.I. and Lil' Wayne

2005

- "Girl"
- "Cater 2 U"
- "Stand Up for Love" (2005 World Children's Day Anthem)

Thank you for reading my book.

I appreciate all of your feedback, and I love hearing what you have to say. I need your input to make the next book in this series better.

Please leave a helpful review wherever you got this copy letting me know what you thought of this book.

Thanks so much!

Who is Harris Rosen?

Father. Son. Brother.

Harris Rosen is the author of **N.W.A: The Aftermath, The Real Eminem: Broke City Trash Rapper**, and other Behind The Music Tales books. For twenty years, he self-published the national lifestyle magazine Peace! He lives in Toronto, Canada, with his son, Louis.

Rosen has interviewed hundreds of composers, artists, actors, and athletes. Including the Notorious B.I.G., Dr Dre, Daft Punk, Eminem, Derek Jeter, Georges St. Pierre, Nirvana, Metallica, Chris Rock, Buju Banton, Beastie Boys, Kiss, Destiny's Child and Aaliyah to list a few.

He has gone to six continents and was in the midst of a whirlwind of multiple musical, cultural revolutions that occurred throughout the 90′s and 2000s while compiling a genuine and honest archive of audio, images and video.

behindthemusictales.com
Facebook: behindthemusictales
Instagram: behindthemusictales
Twitter: mrheller1